Out of the Blue

52 Devotions

By

Jean Peterson

Out of the Blue

52 Devotions

Printed in the United States of America

ISBN: 978-0-9896117-2-5

Gazelle Group of MN, LLC

Forest Lake, Minnesota, U.S.A.

To My Family:

My prayer for each of you is that you would know Him and the power of His resurrection.

Table of Contents

Hello!

I'm so glad to make your acquaintance via the pages of this book. Thanks for taking time out of your busy schedule. It's my hope that as we spend time together in this medium, we'll both experience growth because of it.

You might ask yourself, "So, who are you, Jean, to undertake writing a devotional?"

I'm no one really, just an ordinary woman on a journey with God; a fellow believer whose desire is to love and serve Him with all my heart, mind, soul and strength. I'm a person who has "blown-it-big-time" and yet, been allowed to tell the story of God's redemptive grace. My God is that amazing.

If I could, I'd love to sit with you personally over a cup of coffee enjoying your company and having some great discussions. Scripture says, "As iron sharpens iron, so one person sharpens another." (Prov. 27:17 NIV) In my own life, there are people who challenge me, give me food for thought, and push me to know why I believe what I believe through spiritual dialogue. They're my sharpeners, especially when I don't agree with what they say. I may not always like it, but it's in the sharpening process I become a more finely honed instrument in the service of the King.

If you're not a believer, much of what I say won't make sense. I'm writing from the premise that you are "in a relationship" with Jesus Christ as your Lord and Savior. If that's not you, may I encourage you to take a moment and meet my friend, Jesus? He's the hero in the greatest love story ever told, the Son of God, who was born with the express purpose of reconciliation in mind; the reconciliation of humanity with a God who is crazy in love with us. Crazy in love with ***you***. You see no matter who you are or what you've done, the Bible says "for all have sinned and fallen short of the glory of God."(Romans 3:23 NIV) What's sin? Very simply, the wrong we do. It separates us from God and demands restitution be made. "For the wages of sin is death, but the free gift of God is eternal life through Jesus Christ our Lord." (Romans 6:23 NIV) The good news is Jesus met the demand for restitution and paid the ultimate price, giving His life in exchange for ours, so our fractured relationship with God could be mended. "For God so loved the world that He gave His only begotten Son that whoever believes in Him shall not perish, but have eternal life." (John 3:16 KJV)

Your own love affair begins when you believe what God says is true. You acknowledge the wrong you've done, believe Jesus died on the cross to save you from sin and death, ask for forgiveness, and receive through faith in Jesus, the free gift of salvation. Talk to God. It might sound something like this: "God, I know I've done a lot of things that don't please You. I'm sorry. I'd like to turn that around. I ask You to forgive me. I believe Jesus died on the cross for me so I can be in relationship with You. I come to You now and give You control of my life. Help me to live in way that pleases You. Amen

If you did talk to God just now, may I be the first to welcome you as a brother or sister in Christ. I'd also like to encourage you to get in touch with a local church and let them know of your decision to be in relationship with Jesus. It's important to find other believers to hang around as you start your faith journey. I'd also recommend getting a Bible and reading the Gospel of John. If you don't have or can't afford a Bible, contact a church in your area, I'm sure they'll be happy to help. You can also check out www.Biblegateway.com or www.biblesuite.com for online Bible access. I'm excited you've decided to get to know my God who's crazy in love with you. Your life will never be the same😊

Now, my prayer is that as you read this book, you'll be encouraged, challenged and sharpened. The journey isn't always easy, but the reward is worth it!

Because of Jesus,

Jean

My Intent

My intent in writing this book was to make it a meeting place. Think of it as a coffee or lunch date that you'll put on your calendar once a week for the next year. There are 52 thoughts I'd like to share with you. Some of them you may want to chew on for a while, others may be something you've already digested. Whether these thoughts stick in your teeth, or in your craw, they're meant to encourage spiritual dialogue. They're thoughts I've been chewing on myself, some longer than others.

My prayer is for us to ponder and grow. I'm not a theologian. I'm just an explorer on the adventure of a lifetime. An adventure that really began when I realized this phase of the journey is just the start. If something I say causes you to stretch and grow or sink your roots more deeply into Jesus Christ as your Lord, Savior and Sole Sufficiency, then our time together will have been well spent.

I know there are going to be a few of you out there like me. You're going to read the whole book, cover to cover, in one sitting even though I'd really like to spend the year with you. That's okay. Could I invite you to revisit some of these thoughts when the Lord brings them to your mind? He may have secret treasures tucked away for you that you'll miss in your quest to finish the book.

Regardless of who you are and how you choose to read this book, know this, I'm praying for you. This is my prayer based on Eph 3:16-21, "I ask Father that my brothers and sisters would come to know the riches of Your glory, that You would fill them with the power of Your Holy Spirit, and that Christ would live abundantly in each one of them. I ask for them to know the expanse of Your love; how wide, how high, how deep, how personal and how utterly amazing it is for each one of them. I believe, Lord, You desire to give them life and life abundantly! Thank you for the opportunity we have as a body to encourage and sharpen one another. Let us be willing to learn and grow. Bless them, Lord. In Jesus Name. Amen."

Your Sister in Christ,

Jean

"That He would grant you, according to the riches of His glory to be strengthened with power through His Spirit in the inner man, so that Christ may dwell in your hearts through faith; and that you, being rooted and grounded in love, may be able to comprehend with all the saints what is the breadth and length and height and depth, and to know the love of Christ which surpasses knowledge that you may be filled up to all the fullness of God. Now to Him who is able to do far more abundantly beyond all that we ask or think, according to the power that works within us, to Him be the glory in the church and in Christ Jesus to all generations forever and ever. Amen." (Eph 3:16-21 NASB)

Chapter 1

Have You Ever Had the Feeling?

Have you ever had the feeling God was asking you to do something for which you felt totally inadequate?

I feel that way, right now, with this book.

I've been a Christian for over 30 years. During that time, I've experienced God in various ways at various times. He has always been very "real" in my life ~ yes, I've seen miracles and answers to prayer. My heart's desire, since before my early teens, has been to know Him like Moses knew Him, and speak to Him face to face. I guess you could say that we (God and I) pretty much have an on-going conversation ~ with me mainly asking questions I know I wouldn't even be able to understand the answers to.

I started pushing the issue a couple of years ago when I began to have a sneaking suspicion that the Church, at large, was being robbed of a lot of the truth of what God has for us as believers. So, I began asking God to know the **Truth** ~ His Truth and only His Truth. Not doctrine, not the teachings of man, just Truth. I based my request on two Scripture verses. The first, Jesus' statement in John 8:31-32, "If you abide in My Word, then you are truly disciples of Mine; and you shall know the ***truth*** and the ***truth*** shall set you free." NASB (italics mine) The second scripture was John 14:6, "Jesus said to him, 'I am the way, and the **truth**, and the life; no one comes to the Father but through me." My reasoning was if Jesus is the **truth** (in whom all the fullness of the Godhead dwells) and He promised that by abiding in His Word we would know Him, (the Truth), and be made free, I wanted nothing more than an up close and personal revelation of His Word and Himself as Truth, without all of the static of doctrine and man-made interpretations. I wanted to wipe all the grime of preconceived notions and misconceptions off the windows of my soul and see more clearly the power and fullness of life God has for me in Christ.

So, something has changed over the last few years. My relationship with Him has become more....intense. Jeremiah said "... like a burning fire shut up in my bones and I am weary of holding it in. And I cannot endure it." (Jer. 20:9b NASB) I've got an inkling of what that means now. There are so many things I feel the Lord is speaking and showing me in various ways that I asked Him,"What is it You want me to do with all this 'stuff.' “His response was, "Share it." To which I replied, "Who am I?" His answer, "The one who just talked to me about wanting to walk in obedience." Point, God.

So, here I am, so full of ideas, thoughts, questions, notes, etc. I can hardly contain myself. My hope is that maybe some of my musings, questions, and conversations with God, if you will, will be a benefit to you, my fellow believers.

You may or may not agree with what you read here. That's O.K. I hope my ramblings make you think, dig into Scripture for yourself, and find the Truth of the life God has for you. Remember, this is not about preconceived notions, teachings or beliefs we've long held dear. This is about laying ourselves at the feet of God, and humbly asking Him to open our hearts and minds to the Truth that sets us free, knowing He will give us the strength to walk in it. I look forward to sharing the journey!

Let's pray: Lord, we're asking for your Truth to be revealed to each of us. We surrender our precious beliefs, doctrines and preconceived notions about who You are, how You operate and what You have for us in this life. Stretch us, Lord. Grow us. Challenge us. Burn off the dross, the faulty beliefs, the preconceived notions, anything that is not the truth You want revealed in our lives. We fall at your feet in humble adoration, Lord. You are the Potter and we are the clay. Mold us into what you would have us to be. Let us walk in Your Truth always. In Jesus Name. Amen.

Chapter 2

Taking God at His Word

What would happen if we were to take God at His Word? Literally. What would happen?

I recently read a quote that said, "We must make God's Word our own personal possession. Take any word that He has spoken and say, 'That word is my word.' Put your finger on this promise and say, 'It is mine.' " (Author unknown)

How many of God's promises are we missing out on simply because we have not taken them to heart and believed they were for us, right now, in the midst of whatever circumstance we may be facing? Where we are struggling, do we have the confidence to say, "The Lord's promise is sure. He speaks no careless word; all He says is purest truth, like silver seven times refined?" (Ps 12:6 The Living Bible)

Your situation may be grim. And let's be real ~ there are many of us in unpleasant situations. I'm not saying, as some do, we walk around and say our situations don't exist. I'm saying we find the promises of God that apply to our situations, point to them and say that is God's Word for *me*. It's mine. The God of the Universe gave it to me. He didn't speak it carelessly. And because He spoke it, it is the truth. The truth remains the truth, regardless of what things look like. God's Word is the reality that is to be my life.

Does that mean my life will be a bed of roses? Or that I'll never face any hardship or trial? No. If Christ suffered, who are we too think we will not face some difficult circumstances in our lives? "The servant is not above the Master." Peter tells us in I Peter 4:12-13 "Beloved, do not be surprised at the fiery ordeal among you which comes upon you for your testing, as though some strange thing were happening to you; but to the degree that you share the sufferings of Christ, keep on rejoicing; so that also at the revelation of His glory, you may rejoice with exultation." (NASB) Life happens. Bad things do happen to good people. What's important in these situations is that we place our confidence in God and His promises to us, "knowing that the testing of your faith produces endurance; and let endurance have its perfect result, that you may be perfect and complete lacking in nothing." James 1:3-4 (NASB) We need to come to an understanding in the depths of our being that life's challenges *do not nullify* the promises of God.

Point to the Word in the midst of your difficulties and say, "That promise is mine." Change your paradigm and *take God at His Word,* knowing in the midst of life's circumstances, God's promises for us remain the same. Because, "Jesus Christ is the same yesterday and today, and yes and forever." Heb 13:8 (NASB) Do you need a miracle? God is a God of miracles ~ He hasn't changed. Do you need deliverance? God is the God who delivers ~ He hasn't changed. Wherever you are, whatever you may be facing ~ take God at His Word; apply His promises to your situation. Believe God. And watch what happens.

Let's pray: Lord, please drive into the core of our being that Your promises for us are never made void by our life's circumstances no matter how desperate they may seem. Rather, the challenges we face are opportunities for us to learn what Your promises are and to take You at Your Word. Help us, Lord to see past the veil of this world into the realm of the spirit, and apply the spiritual principles and truths You have for us. There is so much more You intend for us to do and be, open our hearts to those things. In Jesus Name.

Chapter 3

God Gives Us More Than We Can Handle

I've often heard it said, "God never gives you more than you can handle." While I understand the statement is meant to bring comfort ~ I think it's a fundamental misconception in the Christian life. I believe God *loves* to give us more than we can handle. Why? So He can get our attention.

Think about it. When are you most likely to focus on God? When you're living a life of ease and everything is going along just right; or when you're hard pressed from every direction and your world seems to be falling apart? If we're honest, it's during times of crisis, during the times when we can't handle things on our own, we most often cry out to God. Why? Precisely because we're feeling we can't handle whatever is going on by ourselves. We know we need help, so we turn to God.

Lately, it seems there have been numerous brothers and sisters in the Lord who have been facing extremely pressing times in their lives. God is definitely giving them more than they can handle. Marriages are under stress, finances are tight, children are facing and causing challenges of their own, and the list goes on. One sister said, "If things don't ease up soon, I'm going to crack." I think that's exactly what God wants. He wants us to crack. He wants us to acknowledge Him and say, "Lord, there is none beside thee to help." 2 Chron. 14:11 (RV)

We don't learn faith in comfortable surroundings. We don't learn utter dependence upon God when things are going our way. Somehow, it seems we need a little turbulence in our lives every now and again for God to remind us He is the Source of Life, our ever present help in time of trouble. Psalms 46:1, "…God is our refuge and strength, an ever-present help in trouble." (NIV)

I know in my own life, He has used extremely intense and difficult circumstances as a means to an end. And the end, for me, was a surrender so freeing I can hardly describe it. It was and is a surrender that says, "Lord, I'm on the altar. My life is on the altar. Nothing matters except You. Nothing; not family, not finances, not anything this world has to offer. Whatever You have for me is fine. My life is completely Yours, do with it what You will." I've said similar words before and meant them, asking for His guidance, His grace and His will in my life. I've earnestly desired His Presence and the manifestation of the Spirit ~ but this prayer was different. It was from the core of my being, and it's changed my entire perspective on life. I can honestly say if God wants me to live in a cardboard box, I'll be happy to be there as long as I am in the presence of my God. I know I would have voiced a similar sentiment in times past, but there is a difference between a voicing and a knowing. This is a "knowing" from the very depths of my heart. I wish I could describe it more thoroughly, but words fail to describe the depth.

When I asked the Lord about the challenges I was facing and why, He simply said, "You are in the Refiner's fire. It's time to burn off the dross (the impurities) and bring you into a greater understanding of the things I have for you." Wait a minute! I thought I was doing okay. I was walking with God, and doing what I believed I needed to do, and so were the other believers I knew who were going through hard times. But God is a God of Passion, who desires more for us than we even desire for ourselves. He demands that our relationship with Him supersede ALL else. He is jealous of our affections and longs to communicate with us as His beloved. Precisely because He is so passionate, He'll bring us to (and through) the fire in order to purify us in our innermost being and bring us to a place of intimate fellowship with Him. Scripture resounds with this theme.

What is it in your life that you can't handle right now? God has a plan and a purpose for whatever it is. When nothing else is clear, you can cling to this promise. "'For I know the plans I have for you,' says the Lord, 'plans to prosper you and not to harm you, plans to give you hope and a future.'" Jer. 29:11 (NIV)

Let's pray: Lord, thank You that You do give us more than we can handle. As uncomfortable as it is, we know it's because You have more in mind for us than we have in mind for ourselves. Help us to realize when we are in the midst of the fire, You are there. You are with us. You never leave or forsake us. Let the fire be a tool in our lives to bring glory to Your name ~ then, no matter the circumstances, it will be worth it. We love you, Lord. Be it done to us, according to Your Will. In Jesus Name.

Chapter 4

Calling Things That Are Not As Though They Are

I once heard a preacher make what I considered to be a profound statement. He said, "I don't call things that are, as though they are not. I call things that are not as though they are." He was talking about healing and saying that when he is sick he doesn't deny he's sick. Rather, he declares his wellness is what God's promise is and chooses to focus his thoughts and speech in that direction and allow God to bring wellness to him however He sees fit.

We, as children of God, have the right and the privilege to call things that are not as though they are. Romans 4:17 refers to Abraham's faith in God by saying, "As it is written: 'I have made you a father of many nations.' He (Abraham) is our father in the sight of God, in whom he believed—*the God who gives life to the dead and calls things that are not as though they were." NIV* (Italics mine.) You see, God called Abraham "a father of many nations" before he even had a child. God called things that were not yet manifested in the physical world as though they were already done. Chew on that for a while.

As children of God, we are to grow into the image of our Father. Romans 12:2 says, "Do not conform to the pattern of this world, but be transformed by the renewing of your mind. Then you will be able to test and approve what God's will is – His good, pleasing and perfect will." (NIV) If our Father calls things that are not as though they are then we, as His children, need to transform our thinking and begin doing the same. Please hear me clearly. I'm not jumping on the "Name It – Claim It" band wagon. A philosophy that seems to say, "Tell God what you want and Presto! He *has* to give it to you." (God is not a butler at our beck and call.) That's not what I'm saying at all. Any parent knows that you don't give your children everything they ask for, especially if they approach it with a you-have-to-give-it-to-me attitude. What I am saying is, as believers, we've missed a huge piece of the puzzle when it comes to our heritage as children of the Most High God. Think of it like this, when God created this world He spoke it into existence. Read Genesis chapter 1. He said, "Let there be light," and there was light. The light did not exist before He spoke it into existence. Out of nothing, God called things that were not, as though they were. And they were manifest here in the physical world. Because we are created in God's image, we too are given the ability through the Holy Spirit to call things that are not as though they are.

This is the essence of faith. Hebrews 11:1 "What is faith? It is the confident assurance that something we want is going to happen. It is the certainty that what we hope for is waiting for us, even though we cannot see it up ahead." (The Living Bible.)

So, faith essentially calls things that are not as though they are. I was pondering the question of why the church in America doesn't seem to be seeing many miracles and it occurred to me that we lack faith. Both because we don't feel a need and we're simply not used to calling things that are not as though they are. We're much too pragmatic for that. We seem to think what we see is what we get. Yet, that's not what Scripture tells us. Is your brain fried yet?

As I was looking for additional verses on faith, I recalled Jesus' saying in Matt 21:21-22, "Then Jesus told them, 'Truly if you have faith, and don't doubt, you can do things like this and much more. You can even say to this Mount of Olives, 'Move over into the ocean,' and it will. You can get anything - anything you ask for in prayer if you believe." (The Living Bible.) Sound far-fetched? Remember, Jesus also told us we would do greater miracles than He did.

Matthew 17:20 says, "And He said to them, ' Because of the littleness of your faith; for truly I say to you, if you have faith as a mustard seed, you shall say to this mountain, 'Move from here to there, ' and it shall move; and nothing shall be impossible to you." Why? Because all things are possible with God. This is not about us; it's about clearing away the junk and developing a spiritual and eternal perspective that puts the Word of God first and foremost in any and every situation. And when we begin exercising our puny little faith muscles, we need to remember the admonition in James 1:6-8 "But let him ask in faith without any doubting, for the one who doubts is like the surf of the sea driven and tossed by the wind. For let not that man expect that he will receive anything from the Lord, being a double-minded man, unstable in all his ways." (NASB)

If we're going to take God at His word, then we need to believe He meant what He said, not just once in a while, but every time. Whew! That seems like a tall order to me!

Let's be honest here. As I'm wrestling with this whole concept, I can't help but think of the times I've prayed for miracles, healing, restoration, etc. and quite frankly, it seemed like things just went from bad to worse. So, did I not even have "mustard seed" faith? I don't know. What I do know is the problem was most likely with me and my perspective or with the enemy, not with God. God's Word is true, His ways are higher than our ways, and while I may not understand everything that's going on, He's always in control and on the throne. He never changes. All He asks of me is to lay hands on the sick, pray for miracles, and leave the rest up to him. I don't think we can discount the fact that we are in a spiritual battle and the forces of darkness do wage war. (Although, I don't think they've had to do too much work in this area, because we don't seem to be taking it too seriously.) But one of the great weapons of warfare from "the dark side" is simply to "let sleeping dogs lie." If Christians don't walk in faith, take God at His Word, and call things that are not as though they are, (Basically, ask for and expect to receive miracles) how much work does Satan really have to do? None. Point, Satan. Secondly, I am profoundly convinced that we, as a body, are not saturated in the Word of God. How can I believe, claim or pray His promises if I don't know them personally? God's Word needs to be oozing out of my pores as the essence of my very being. When that happens my prayers are going to align with His will, most likely changing from me from my selfish "gimme gimme" prayers to requests that pierce the Father's heart and move His hand.

So, where do I go with all of this? For myself, I know I need to soak in more of God's promises. I need to step out in faith and start talking to those mountains. I need to call those things that are not as though they are in accordance with God's Word. I need to find my little mustard seed, plant it and help it grow, so I can fulfill the promise of doing greater miracles for the Kingdom.

Let's pray: Lord, this question of faith is one with which I wrestle. I want to call things that are not as though they are in accordance with Your will. Help me to understand, to rightly divide Your word, to walk in obedience, and to accept Your promises. I know, Lord, this is not about me, it's about Your Kingdom, Your love and Your desire that none should perish. Help me to walk in faith. Develop that mustard seed in me. Let me do greater things so You receive the glory! In Jesus Name. Amen.

Chapter 5

Diamonds Are Formed Under Incredible Pressure

I'm wondering where we ever got the idea if we turned our lives over to the Lord things were going to be easy. I know there are times when it seems as if the world is crashing in around me and I look up at the Lord and say, "It's not supposed to be this way!" Really? If I take an honest look at the Scriptures, it seems to me God's greatest leaders have always gone through times of intense trial. Look at Joseph - sold as a slave and thrown in prison through no fault of his own, Moses - ripped from the luxury of Egypt's palaces to tend sheep in the desert, David - hunted by the Saul because of Saul's jealousy, Daniel - thrown into the lion's den because of his devotion to God. So, who am I to think I should bypass the trials in life?

God never promised there wouldn't be trials. In fact, He says the exact opposite - "in this world you will have trouble, but take heart, I have overcome the world." John 16:33 (NIV)

And David says, "Yea, though I walk through the valley of the shadow of death, I will fear no evil, for Thou art with me. Thy rod and thy staff, they comfort me."Ps 23:4 (KJV) I think that means we'll walk through valleys, because valleys are part of the journey. But as we're walking in them, we'll know God is walking with us through the difficulty and using it to accomplish His purpose in our lives.

In fact, we know more than that. We know God uses our trying times to forge our character into what He intends it to be. Trouble has a way of refining and defining us. It's in the heat of affliction our true character shines through. What's our first thought when trouble comes? Do we turn to God, fall on our knees and recognize He is our only source, our sole sufficiency, or do we complain, curse and whine? Really, what is your response to testing times?

A diamond is only formed under intense heat and pressure. It's through extreme conditions that the molecular structure of the diamond is melded into place. And it's the molecular structure, the bonds at the very core of the stone that make the diamond what it is. The bonds of a diamond have such integrity of purpose that it's the hardest substance known to man. A diamond can cut through every other substance. I think God longs to form integrity of purpose in our belief and faith infrastructure like those formed in a diamond. The only way He can accomplish this is to let us go through times of intense pressure. The hardships in our lives are the only way He can remake us in the most elemental part of our being. I believe His desire is to form such integrity of conviction and faith in us that we become impenetrable. As we are transformed in this manner, I also believe we become brilliant to behold ~

just like a diamond; so we can "...shine as lights in the midst of a dark and perverse generation." (My paraphrase of Phil 2:15 NASB)

We are diamonds in the rough. Some just beginning to become diamonds in the midst of intense trials, some have an internal structure formed, but now must go through the mining process, and some are ready to be cut and reveal the brilliance of the lessons learned in the times of trial. It really doesn't matter where we are on the journey. What's important to know is God is at work, even when we don't see how He could be in view of our situation. When we understand God is at work in the trials of our lives, our troubles will take on a different meaning for us and we'll be able to "give thanks in everything." (I Thess 5:18)

As I'm writing this, I'm reminded of a devotional I read a while back in a book called "Streams in the Desert." Part of that devotional read, "Tribulation is the way to triumph. The valley-way opens into the highway. Tribulation's imprint is on all great things. Crowns are cast in crucibles. Chains of character that wind about the feet of God are forged in earthly flames. No man is greatest victor till he has trodden the winepress of woe. With seams of anguish deep in His brow, the 'Man of Sorrows' said, 'Be of good cheer, I have overcome the world.' The footprints are traceable everywhere. Blood marks stain the steps that lead to thrones. Scars are the price of scepters. Our crowns will be wrested from the giants we conquer. Grief has always been the lot of greatness. It is an open secret, 'The mark of rank in nature is capacity for pain; and the anguish of the singer makes the sweetest strain.'

Tribulation has always marked the trail of the true reformer. It is the story of Paul, Luther, Savonarola, Know, Wesley, and all the rest of the mighty army. They came through great tribulation to their place of power." *Streams in the Desert*

So, don't be surprised at the great trials and pressures in your life. God is using them to create something wonderful in you. For a while it may seem unbearable, but the results will be beautiful to behold!

Let's Pray: Lord, help us to realize in the midst of our trials, You are working. You're forging in us integrity of character that cannot be overcome by this world. You're causing us to become more than conquerors, because we choose to acknowledge You as Lord in every circumstance and situation. Take me as a diamond in the rough, and do whatever is necessary to create a brilliant reflection of Your glory in my life. I love You, Lord. Amen

Chapter 6
High Treason

I once heard a speaker say, "If we're not walking out our calling in the Kingdom, we are guilty of high treason." Wow! That pierced my heart and made me sit back and take stock of my own walk with God.

I don't think walking in your calling is the easiest thing God will ask you to do, but it will definitely be the most fulfilling! I can relate to Moses when he said, in effect, "Here am I ~ send Aaron." (See Exodus 3 for the story.) We can all look around and see others who seem infinitely more qualified for the job. Moses had a problem speaking, so Aaron seemed the more logical choice. But we need to keep a couple of things in mind when we're looking at our own calling and what it is God has asked us to do. First, His thoughts are not our thoughts and His ways are not our ways. (Is. 55:8) Secondly, He chose the foolish things of the world to shame the wise and the weak things of the world to shame the strong. (I Cor. 1:27) God uses shepherd boys, slaves and prisoners (Joseph, Daniel, and

Apostle Paul) to accomplish His purposes, as long as they're willing to listen.

When I was questioning God about some things I felt He had laid on my heart to do, I was quick to point out a few areas where I felt I was lacking a specific skill that I would need to succeed. I felt God saying, "Good. Then, it's not about you, is it? Because when I accomplish my purpose through you, you'll know it wasn't you, it was Me. I'm not asking you to be perfect; I'm asking you to be obedient." Ouch! If it boils down to obedience, then I'm left with no excuses. Either I will or I won't ~ it's my choice. Since I know obedience is better than sacrifice, (I Sam 15:22) it would seem that it's high time to get with it!

I think I need to come to a deeper understanding of what the Apostle Paul knew. "When I am weak, then I am strong." (II Cor. 12:10) I need to throw myself with utter abandon into the call God has placed on my life. (And on every believer's life.) If you're a believer, you have a call, a destiny and a purpose in God's Kingdom. You see, in Christian circles, we have relegated a "call" to those who are in obvious ministry positions – pastors, missionaries, evangelists, etc. People whose vocation it is to do "God-things." But we all have a call; a job to do. Ask God what it is and then get busy. It might be building a business, it might be parenting foster kids, it might be preaching, it might be interceding, it might be working in an elder care facility, or doing any number of things....but God has something He wants you to do. Are you doing it? Or are you guilty of treason?

Let's Pray: Lord, help us to step confidently into our calling. Open our hearts and minds to what it is You want us to do, then equip us to do it. We want to advance Your Kingdom here on Earth. We want to be vessels of Your Glory. Teach us how, Lord. Give us willing hearts. In Jesus Name.

Chapter 7

Speak Life

Have you ever considered the power of the tongue and the words you speak? Proverbs 18:21 states, "The tongue has the power of life and death, and those who love it will eat its fruit." (NIV) The New Century Version says, "What you say can mean life or death. Those who speak with care will be rewarded." So, think about the words you've used today, have they caused life or death? More importantly, what is your standard pattern of speech day in and day out? Do you spend time proclaiming the truths of God, or are you buying into the lies of the enemy and moaning the world is going to hell in a hand basket and there's nothing we can do about it.

People of God, in the midst of challenging and turbulent times shouldn't we be the harbingers of hope to a lost and dying world? I'm not saying we don't acknowledge gas prices are on the rise, families are struggling and the economy is tough to say the least. What I am saying is we, as the people of God, have the right, duty and privilege to speak life into this dying world, because we know the Author of Life, Jesus!

Our God is the God who calls "things that are not as though they are." Romans 4:17. For instance, "Then God ***said***, 'Let there be light' ~ and there was light." Gen1:3. He spoke, and the light that did not exist before He spoke came into existence. God called things that were not as though they were. Now, bear with me here. How many things have we spoken into existence, whether positive or negative, that we aren't even aware of because we're not aware of the power of our words? And how many things should we be speaking into existence based on the promises of God, which we are not?

I'm sure many of you are aware of the phenomenon of "The Secret." Essentially, it's a teaching stating that via your thoughts and your speech you materialize, or manifest, your reality here in this dimension as the result of the "universe" responding to you. So, if you've got negative stuff in your life, you "attracted" it either subconsciously or consciously and all you need to do is change your core thought process and then focus on and align your speech with what it is you really want. The proponents of this teaching are close, but they neglect to acknowledge God, not the universe, is the source, and Jesus is the Truth we must seek. They're right in saying a person needs to change their thought and speech patterns, but they don't realize our thought and speech patterns need to find some format to follow. Man left to himself, does not reach for good; he reaches for evil. We need to wrap our thoughts around the promises of God, because His Word is Truth. David said in 2 Samuel 7:28, "For You are indeed God, and Your words are truth, and You have promised me these good things...." We need to speak God's truths to a lost and dying world. But, I don't think we can do that effectively until we have appropriated those truths for ourselves. And we can't grasp the truths God has for us apart from the Holy Spirit because Jesus said, "He is the Holy Spirit, the Spirit who leads into all truth." John 14:17 So where does that leave us?

I believe we need to immerse ourselves in the Word of God and ask the Holy Spirit to show us the truths within. We need to know the promises, rights and privileges we have as children of the King. Then, we need to begin to speak life, speak those promises, and call things that are not as though they are. Because if we are children of the King we should be acting like the King, and the King and God I see revealed in Scripture loves to speak life! He speaks the truth that leads to life. Whether or not we decide to act upon the truth He speaks is our choice.

I think it saddens God when we operate in a negative mindset while grumbling and complaining about our circumstances and what's going on in the world around us. Don't get me wrong, I'm not saying we act like everything is fine and deny what is. I'm saying we take a spiritual stand, look into the Word of God, speak the truths laid out in Scripture and call things that are not as though they are. Because they *are* if God said they are! We just don't see them yet. That is the essence of faith. Knowing that something we want is going to happen, the certainty that something we hope for is waiting for us, even though we cannot see it up ahead. (Heb 11:1)

We need to take it upon ourselves to speak life by speaking the truths of God in the midst of a lost and dying world. We need to speak God's truths to ourselves and we need to speak them to those around us. The truths we speak may not always be pretty or popular, but they should always lead to life. And they should always be spoken in love.

Let's Pray: Lord, help us to speak life. Reveal Your Truth to us through the work of the Holy Spirit in our lives. Let us walk in the power of Your promises. Make us wise to the schemes of the enemy and don't let us lend power to his operation by the words that come out of our mouths. Put a guard on our lips, Lord. Teach us Your paths and let us bring life through the words we speak to ourselves, to our families and friends, and to a lost and dying world. We love you, Lord. Amen.

Chapter 8

God Is Never In A Hurry

I just finished reading a devotional from "Streams in the Desert." It struck me that it may be helpful to many of my brothers and sisters who are in the midst of trying circumstances. I know it challenged me and gave me hope. So, here is the devotion I read.

'And when forty years were expired, there appeared to him in the wilderness of Mount Sinai an angel of the Lord in a flame of fire in a bush....saying...I have seen the affliction of my people which is in Egypt, and I have heard their groaning, and am come down to deliver them. And now come, I will send thee to Egypt.' (Acts 7:30, 32, 34 KJV)

'That was a long wait in preparation for a great mission. When God delays, He is not inactive. He is getting ready His instruments, He is ripening our powers: and at the appointed moment we shall arise equal to our task. Even Jesus of Nazareth was thirty years in privacy, growing in wisdom before He began His work.' - Dr. Jowett

'God is never in a hurry but spends years with those He expects to greatly use. He never thinks the days of preparation too long or too dull.

'The hardest ingredient in suffering is often time. A short, sharp pang is easily borne, but when a sorrow drags its weary way through long, monotonous years, and day after day returns with the same dull routine of hopeless agony, the heart loses its strength, and without the grace of God, is sure to sink into the very sullenness of despair. Joseph's was a long trial, and God often has to burn His lessons into the depths of our being by the fires of protracted pain. 'He shall sit as a refiner and purifier of silver,' but He knows how long, and like a true goldsmith He stops the fires the moment He sees His image in the glowing metal. We may not see now the outcome of the beautiful plan which God is hiding in the shadow of His hand; it yet may be long concealed; but faith may be sure that He's is sitting on the throne, calmly waiting the hour when, with adoring rapture, we shall say, 'All things have worked together for good.' There is a 'need-be' for every lesson, and when we are ready, our deliverance will surely come, and we shall find that we could not have stood in our place of higher service without the very things that were taught us in the ordeal. God is educating us for the future, higher service and nobler blessings; and if we have the qualities that fit us for a throne, nothing can keep us from it when God's time has come. *Don't steal tomorrow out of God's hands. (Italics mine)* Give God time to speak to you and reveal His will. He is never too late; learn to wait.'" Devotional from "Streams in the Desert."

Brothers and sisters who are living in the trials of fire ~ you are not alone! There are others who are also walking paths of protracted pain. Take heart, it's not because you've done wrong and you are being punished, it's that God has a higher calling and purpose for which He is preparing you! You are beloved of God! He is holding you in the palm of His hand! And He is carefully forging the character in you that you need to accomplish the work He has set before you. You are in the Refiner's fire because He desires to produce His finest work in you. Will you allow Him too?

Let's Pray: Lord, open our hearts and minds to the plans you have for us; plans to prosper us, not to harm us, even when we feel the searing heat from the flames of Your Refiner's fire. Your desire is for our best; and for that to happen, we need to come to the point of complete surrender and unquestioning obedience. Lord, I give You permission to bend my stubborn heart and melt my iron will into whatever will be useful in service to You and Your kingdom. What I have to offer is not pretty, or of great worth, but your Son bought it with His blood, and I humbly offer my life back to You as a living sacrifice. In Jesus Name. Amen

Chapter 9

What Do You Have In Your Hand?

Have you ever said that you'll start doing big things for God when.... the house is paid off, the kids are off to college, the retirement fund is padded, you make it big...etc., etc.? It's almost as if we hold up a hushing finger to God's plans for our lives and say, we'll do it when we feel we're in a comfortable enough spot to turn our attention to the things God wants us to do. Could that be the reason so many of us feel like we're on a hamster wheel, running as fast as we can, but getting nowhere?

We've got it backwards!! God says, "Seek ye first the Kingdom of God and His righteous and all these things shall be added to you." Matt. 6:33 (KJV) Then, He asks, "What do you have in your hand?" Remember the boy with the loaves and fishes? God didn't ask the disciples to go out, work hard and get enough to feed the hungry crowd under their own power, He simply asked them, "What do you have in your hand?" Meaning what do you have that's available for Me to use right now to meet the need and do the ministry that needs to be done? It doesn't have to be big. And you certainly don't have to go out and get "enough" of whatever for God to use. He wants to know what you have, right now, that you're willing to put into His hands for His glory. Is it an unused talent, a bank account, a way with people, a meal you can prepare, or a loaf of bread and some fish? Whatever it is, when we turn it over to God it will be more than enough to accomplish His work.

I can hear some of you saying, "But I don't have anything!" Neither did the widow with the mite. But she gave all she had. And the widow that Elisha helped was about to have her sons taken away to pay the family debt. She had less than nothing! "And Elisha said to her, 'What shall I do for you? Tell me, what do you have in the house?' And she said, "Your maidservant has nothing in the house except a jar of oil.' Then he said, 'Go, borrow vessels at large for yourself from all you neighbors, even empty vessels; do not get a few. And you shall go in and shut the door behind you and your sons, and pour out into all these vessels; and you shall set aside what is full.' So she went from him and shut the door behind her and her sons; they were bringing the vessels to her and she poured. And it came about when the vessels were full, that she said to her son, 'Bring me another vessel.' And he said to her, 'There is not one vessel more.' And the oil stopped. Then she came and told the man of God. And he said, 'Go, sell the oil and pay your debt, and you and your sons can live on the rest.' "(2 Kings 4:2-7 NASB)

When we're willing to put what we have (whether it's a lot, a little, or less than nothing) in God's hands, He will move. It's not about us. It's about God showing Himself strong through us in our obedience. Are you willing to put what you have in your hand today at the feet of the Master?

Let's Pray: Lord, we get so caught up in needing to have "things" to serve you. Yet, you've never asked us for things. You've always said it's obedience you want. It's a heart that says, all I am and all I have is Yours, Lord. There's no part of me I withhold. I choose You this day, and ask You to use what I have in my hand, be it little or be it much, please use it to Your glory. In Jesus Name. Amen.

Chapter 10

Thy Will Be Done

I was thinking about The Lord's Prayer the other day as I was driving along. Since The Lord's Prayer is what Jesus prayed when His disciples asked Him to teach them to pray, I decided to look it up and read it again.

Here are a couple of the thoughts I had while I was reading. Mt. 6:9 - 13 (NASB)

"Our Father who art in heaven, hallowed be thy name." I wonder just how much reverence I do give God's name on a daily basis. Here Jesus starts His prayer in humility of heart, reminding us that while Christ purchased the right for us to come into the throne room and present ourselves before the God of the Universe, we are to do so as grateful children and not spoiled brats who demand instead of request.

"Thy kingdom come. Thy will be done, on earth as it is in heaven." For some reason, this phrase has been hanging with me. "Thy will be done, on earth as it is in heaven." How is God's will done in heaven? I would imagine with immediacy,

urgency, and awe. Can you imagine an angel saying, "Yeah, God...I'll get to that in a minute, OK?" Yet, isn't that an attitude that can creep into our lives? I'll do it when I've got time, God. I felt convicted of my own lack of urgency in some things I know God has spoken to me. If I can't imagine angels not acting immediately, how dare I put off the Creator of the Universe when He requests something of me? Thank God for His mercy and grace!

"Give us this day our daily bread." I was reminded of Israel in the desert when God fed them with manna. Exodus 16:4 - 5 " Then the Lord said to Moses, 'Behold, I will rain bread from heaven for you; and the people shall go out and gather a day's portion every day, that I may test them, whether or not they will walk in my instruction. And it will come about on the sixth day, when they prepare what they bring in, it will be twice as much as they gather daily." (NASB) God provided bread (manna) daily for the children of Israel. And He did it in order to see whether or not they would follow His instructions! Did Jesus only show us to ask for our daily bread, so we would be reminded of our dependence upon God to supply our needs each and every day? And as God supplies our needs, will we walk in the instructions He gives to us regarding His provision?

"And forgive us our debts, as we also have forgiven our debtors." Be careful when you pray this! Think about it, how have you forgiven people? Partially, not at all, or in some other form of "forgiveness" that really isn't forgiveness at all? How do you want your debts to be forgiven? I know I need to take a deep, honest look at how I forgive people, because if I want to be forgiven as I forgive, I need to make sure how I forgive lines up with the Word of God, so I can experience His complete

blessing. God forgave me completely and without reservation. Should I do any less for those I need to forgive?

"And do not lead us into temptation, but deliver us from evil." Jesus was tempted, so He understands the conflict it can cause in us. I think He asked for us to be delivered from evil from the perspective of one who's wrestled with Satan face to face.

"For Thine is the kingdom and the power and the glory forever. Amen." Yes, Lord, Yours is the kingdom, and the power, and the glory forever!!!!

Let's Pray: Lord, You taught us how to pray. And You often went away alone to pray. It's time with the Father that brings us to the place we should be. Show us who You are Lord. Teach us to walk in Your ways. Help us to exalt Your name in all that we do. Lord, we love you. Amen.

Chapter 11
A Place of Breaking Through

As I was reading in I Chronicles 14 about David as he entered the calling God had for him to be king of Israel, a couple of things struck me. First, it took a while, years actually, before God's promise that David would be king was fulfilled. I think those years David served Saul, and then hid from him in the desert were years of preparation. Secondly, verse 11 in chapter 14 seemed to jump out at me. It says, "So he attacked them at Baal-perazim and wiped them out. He exulted, 'God has used me to sweep away my enemies like water bursting through a dam!' That is why the place has been known as Baal-perazim ever since (meaning, 'The Place of Breaking Through.')(Living Bible) Baal-perazim also means the Lord who breaks out.

I need a Baal-perazim place in my life right now. I need the Lord who breaks out to move on my behalf. And I know there are many of my brothers and sisters who do as well. We need to be at the Place of Breaking Through to see God's promises come to pass. We need to not be weary, but continue to fight the good fight. We need to see the enemy swept away like water bursting through a dam.

Sometimes it seems as if the breaking through times in our lives don't come soon enough for us, especially when the promises we have from God seem to be delayed or forgotten. Years in the desert, God? I'm supposed to be king! You've called me into business? Why the delay? Or I'm supposed to be ________, you fill in the blank. Remember, Beloved, God is not slow in fulfilling His promises. He simply operates on a different timeline than we do. "...With the Lord one day is as a thousand years, and a thousand years as one day." (2 Peter 3:8 KJV) In the end, there is always a Baal-perazim - a place of breaking through. Abraham experienced it when he was about to sacrifice Isaac. Joseph experienced it after slavery and imprisonment. David experienced it as he went to battle as Israel's newly appointed king. Job experienced it when God restored his fortunes and increased them twofold. Jesus experienced it when he rose from the dead. There is always a Baal-perazim!

Your Baal-perazim will come. But, it will come in God's time, not yours. Are you willing to trust Your Heavenly Father knowing He knows what you need before you even need it? Are you willing to rest in His Presence knowing when the time is not just right, but perfect, you will have your breakthrough? It's not easy waiting for the breakthrough. But we can be confident in God's faithfulness. He will provide.

Let's Pray: Lord, there are brothers and sisters, including myself who need a Baal-perazim, a place of breaking through, physically, emotionally, spiritually, financially. Whatever the need Lord, I earnestly seek the breakthrough. Show yourself to be the Commander of the Armies of Heaven and march out on behalf of your people. Break through the strongholds of the enemy. Run on the walls and bring great victories to Your people so Your name will be glorified! Use us, Lord, in the battle. And help us to fight the good fight of faith. We love you, Lord! Amen.

Chapter 12

Talking To Mountains

Call me crazy, but I've been talking to a lot of mountains lately. You heard me, talking to mountains: mountains of apathy, mountains of financial crisis, mountains of physical illness, mountains of spiritual strongholds and darkness, and mountains of....well, just about anything. There are a lot of circumstances in my own life and in the lives of my brothers and sisters looming like mountains ~ huge, overpowering, and intimidating. So why am I talking to them you ask? Well, it occurred to me one day as I was driving along, Jesus said I could. So, I decided I would!

Mt.21:21-22, "And Jesus answered and said to them, 'Truly I say to you, if you have faith, and do not doubt, you shall not only do what was done to the fig tree, but even if you say to this mountain, 'Be taken up and cast into the sea,' it shall happen. And all things you ask in prayer, believing, you shall receive." (NASB)

There's the whole believing, (faith) issue again. It seems I keep circling back around to believing. Do I believe what God said in His Word is true for me today? I know I do. If that's so, then how can I best act in agreement with His Word and bring myself into alignment with what God says is true? Well, I decided to start talking to mountains as just one of the ways I could begin to apply God's Word in my life. And, you know what? I'm seeing mountains begin to move! (How could I have thought any differently?) I'm not saying there's not a struggle. I'm not saying life is all peaches and cream. I'm saying, I have a right and a duty to talk to mountains and have them move! You can talk to mountains too.

So, what mountain in your life needs talking to? Are you ready to tell it to be taken up and cast into the sea? Are you open to believing God can do whatever He wants to in your situation and He can easily deliver should He so choose? Our God is bigger than any mountain. There is nothing too hard for Him. I think that's something we need to keep in mind during these turbulent times. God moves mountains and gives His people the peace that passes all understanding to guard our hearts and minds. He's got everything under control.

Let's Pray: Lord, You are the Mover of Mountains, nothing is impossible with You. There is nothing too hard for You. But, Lord, I often lose sight of that fact. Forgive my unbelief! Let me set roots that drink deeply from the knowledge of Your ways. Open my mind to Your infinite truths.

Father, I speak to the mountains in my life and in the lives of so many brothers and sisters and ask they be taken up and cast into the sea so Your name will be glorified. Set your people apart, and guard us as the apple of Your eye. Be to us a great protecting rock to which we can run in times of trouble. Help us to walk in truth and righteousness, boldly and without reservation. We love You, Lord! May Your Name be glorified!

Chapter 13

Troubled Times?

It seems I can't go anywhere without hearing someone say how desperate the times are, how bleak things look, or how tough things are, or that we can only expect things to get worse. I realize it's fear talking in most instances; fear of the unknown, of hunger, of lack, and of who knows what else. Dear friends, we need to remember God has not given us a spirit of fear and we ought not to be operating from that mind set. II Tim 1:7, "For God has not given us a spirit of timidity, but a spirit of power, love and self discipline."(NASB)

God promises to supply all our needs according to His riches in glory. (Not all our wants, mind you, but our needs.) I've personally experienced His miraculous provision throughout the course of my life. When I needed tuition money in Bible College, when I needed a job, when I wanted a saddle for my horse but only had a certain amount of money, God has always been faithful. It's not that I haven't worried or wondered or cried out in frustration. It's that God's Word is true, His promises are sure and it's up to me to know what those promises are so that when it seems like the world is falling apart around me, I can walk by faith (by believing) in the promises of God. God is faithful. He always has been and always will be. So, if you're feeling a little overwhelmed by the world right now, take a look at Ps. 91 in the Living Bible. It starts out, "We live within the shadow of the Almighty, sheltered by the God who is above all gods. This I declare, that He alone is my refuge, my place of safety; He is my God, and I am trusting Him. For He rescues you from every trap, and protects you from the fatal plague. He will shield you with His wings! They will shelter you. His faithful promises are your armor. Now you don't need to be afraid of the dark anymore, nor fear the dangers of the day; nor dread the plagues of darkness, nor disaster in the morning....."

So, brothers and sisters, we have a great opportunity before us. As the world panics, we can walk in the peace that passes all understanding; being as innocent as doves, yet as wise as serpents. We need to recognize when the spirit of fear is affecting us and then speak to ourselves what God has promised. Mind you, it's not a magical cure for whatever ails us, but we need to continually remind ourselves God is in control. Our outlook should be different than those around us who don't know the King of Kings and the Lord of Lords. And others should easily see us walking to the beat of a different drummer. Our peace and joy should cause them to ask, what's different about us. Then, we need to be ready to give an answer.

Let's pray: Lord, help us to live peace filled lives in the midst of the difficulties of the world, so we can be witnesses of Your promises and provision. Forgive us our unbelief, and help us to walk to walk in Your Spirit. In Jesus name. Amen.

Chapter 14

Road Kill

Ever feel like "road kill?" You know, squashed flat and pounded into the pavement. Wishing someone would just scoop you up and dump you in the ditch before the next semi comes along and flattens you even more. I've felt like that. There have been some hard times in my family and my finances some caused by me, some caused by the actions of others. Much of the time, during these circumstances, life seemed very bleak. So, when we're on the "road kill" side of life, what do we do?

I know I spent a lot of time crying, praying, and seeking the Lord. I knew ultimately, no matter how I felt or how desperate my circumstances seemed, God doesn't change. He is the same yesterday, today and forever. That means He's still in control, even when I feel like everything is spinning out of control in my life. Then, as I was reading, I came across this verse in Psalm 3:3 - 6, "But Lord, You are my shield, my glory, and my only hope. You alone can lift my head now bowed in shame. I cried to the Lord, and He heard me from his Temple in Jerusalem. Then I lay down and slept in peace and woke up safely, for the Lord was watching over me. And now, although ten thousand enemies surround me on every side, I am not afraid."

It felt like 10,000 enemies surrounding me, or like a line of 10,000 semi trucks waiting to rev their engines and run over me with all 18 wheels. But, God loves to lift us up! God loves to shut the lions' mouths! God loves to deliver us and turn our ashes into beauty! He is the God of restoration, even when we've blown it. He's ready to forgive and walk through the fall out with us. As long as I've walked with God (over 47 years) I've always been amazed at His grace, His forgiveness and love. We all make mistakes. The key is to confess our faults to God, turn around and walk in the opposite direction of whatever behavior or decision we made that flattened us in the first place. Then, I suggest getting together with brothers and sisters in the Body of Christ and letting them help you pray it through. There's power in prayer and there's power in numbers.

Let's pray: Lord, I feel like road kill today. But I know with You all things are possible. I know in You as I confess my faults, sins and failings, I am made new through the blood of Christ. Thank You for Your grace, thank You for Your mercy, and thank You for the lessons learned and the victories that will be forthcoming from my failures in life. My heart's desire is in every circumstance and in every situation, You would be glorified. I know You are a God who makes all things new. Bring newness to my life that will bring glory and honor to You and You alone. In Jesus Name. Amen

Chapter 15

To Obey or Not To Obey ~ That Is the Question

To obey or not to obey, that is the question. It's actually not a question at all, but a life lesson God seems to be continually driving home to me, especially recently. Tonight, for instance, I was scheduled to sing special music at my church. I was excited and had a song picked out and rehearsed and was praying about it the night before I was to sing. It was at that time, I felt the Lord say," I want you to sing the chorus "'Blessed Be Your Name.' "I promptly replied, "But I already practiced this other song."

"Sing - Blessed Be Your Name."

"But I already practiced this other song."

To which the Lord replied, "Do you want to argue, or do you want to obey?"

"Hmmmmm....let me see.....okay God, You win."

I sang, "Blessed Be Your Name." It wasn't the greatest rendition, but it was a rendition of obedience and it was meant from the heart. After service a woman approached me and said, "I really needed to hear that song tonight." Wow. God is an amazing God!

In I Samuel 15:22 it says, "But Samuel replied, 'Does the Lord delight in burnt offerings and sacrifices as much as in obeying the voice of the Lord? To obey is better than sacrifice and to heed is better than the fat of rams." I think the original song I was going to sing would have been a meaningless burnt offering if I had ignored God and gone ahead and sung it anyway. What do you think? I wonder just how many times I'm acting with good intentions, but without the obedience in my life that God desires. When I do that, I think God sighs and begins scraping at the black gunk on the grill of my life so He can show me what really matters.

Earlier this month, I had a similar conversation with the Lord. (What can I say? I'm one of God's hard-headed kids.) I was standing in a prayer meeting and one of the ministers was praying for people. He came and prayed for me and I turned to go sit down. The Lord told me to wait, that He was going to send the minister back. "Uh, Lord, everyone else is sitting down, and the minister hasn't come back to pray a second time over anyone else. I'm really going to look stupid standing here all by myself. Could I just go sit down? "

"No, I want you to wait."

"But Lord, I feel really silly standing here and..."

"Do you want to argue? Or do you want to obey?"

So, I stood, and before the minister was done at the side of the auditorium he was ministering on, he turned and came straight back to me with a specific word and prayer! I'm sure God was up there going..DUH! (Don't worry - He's used to it where I'm concerned.) I'm glad I'm slowly learning to heed and obey. I'm thankful for God's patience as I muddle through my life trying to do what He wants me to do. It should be simple, but in my humanity, I complicate things. Thankfully, my God is merciful, slow to anger and rich in love!

Let's Pray: Lord, clearly, you want me to obey. Forgive me for my stubbornness and my independent spirit. Help me to listen for Your voice. Let me act obediently on what I hear. Help me to know and feel Your heart for what's important to You in my life. It's all on the altar. May it be a sacrifice that is holy and acceptable to You. In Jesus Name.

Chapter 16

Faith That Moves Mountains

I wrote a while back about talking to mountains and for some reason; I seem to be circling back around to that subject. Interestingly enough, I came across Mt. 21: 21-22 in my daily reading yesterday. Here it is:" Jesus answered, 'I tell you the truth, if you have faith and do not doubt, you will be able to do what I did to this tree and even more. You will be able to say to this mountain, 'Go, fall into the sea.' And if you have faith, it will happen. If you believe, you will get anything you ask for in prayer." NCV

Then, "coincidentally," I received Dr. Dan Erickson's encouragement for the day this morning. He was talking about unforgiveness, but here is a quote from his blog," I was recently reading from Mark 11:22-25, which is related to this topic. The passage starts off with a bang: "Have faith in God." We can have faith in God that his promises are true, that he does not lie."

This is the full Scripture Dr. Dan is referring to: "Jesus answered, 'Have faith in God. I tell you the truth, you can say to this mountain, 'Go, fall into the sea.' And if you have no doubts in your mind and believe that what you say will happen, God will do it for you. So I tell you to believe that you have received the things you ask for in prayer, and God will give them to you. When you are praying, if you are angry with someone, forgive him so that your Father in heaven will also forgive your sins." Mk 11:22-25 NCV

My prayer lately has been that I would know Truth, because God promises the Truth will set us free. Jesus said in both of these passages, that He told us the truth. (And that is all He can do because He is Truth.) And the truth He told us is, if we do not doubt and we believe we have received what we ask for, God will give it to us. It's rather mind boggling when you think of it. So, where does this equation break down in my own life? Somewhere between where the Holy Spirit in me says, "Yes! Yes! That's it!" and where my humanity looks at my here and now "reality" with all its looming mountains.

Einstein once said, "Reality is merely an illusion, albeit a very persistent one." So what I need to realize is that my reality is not necessarily God's reality. His view of my life and my view of my life, and the mountains in it, are dramatically different. God looks at my life outside of the confines of space and time; in fact, outside of everything I consider to be "reality," those things I can see, hear, feel, touch and experience. It's not those things don't matter, they do, but there is a far greater reality than I can truly comprehend. The reality in which my God lives is eternal and incomprehensible to me.

You see, I tend to doubt that which is not in my immediate realm of experience. And when I do, I doubt what God has told me to be true. If I am in a place of doubt, then I'm actually questioning His integrity, am I not? I'm saying, "I know You said this, God, but...." James says, "Such doubters are thinking two different things at the same time, and they cannot decide about anything they do. They should not think that they will receive anything from the Lord." (James 1:7-8) It's rather prideful of me to doubt God isn't it? It means I'm saying, "Yeah, God, I'm pretty uncertain about this. I'm not sure I can believe what You say, because after all, it's pretty unlikely." WOW! Who am I to even begin to question the Sovereign Lord of the Universe? Yet, I do it all the time!! My flesh and my spirit are constantly in a tug-of-war over the "truth."

So here's what I know. The Truth that reigns supreme is God's truth. Nothing more, nothing less. It doesn't matter what my perception of reality might be at any given time. God's Truth doesn't change. He is the same yesterday, today, and forever. So, if there are mountains that need to be moved, I need to go to God in prayer believing He will move them. I need to know the how and the when are not up to me. The praying and the taking God at His Word are my part in the equation.

Let's Pray: Help me, Lord, to see my life through Your eyes, from Your perspective and Your reality. Let me see these mountains as You see them. Help me to know the Truth, because You promise the Truth will set me free! I have some mountains in my life that need to be moved, Lord. I know of several brothers and sisters with mountains in their lives as well. I ask for the mountains to be moved in such a way that You receive the glory and we learn the lessons they are meant to teach us. We do believe, Lord. Help our unbelief. Draw us ever closer to Your heart. In Jesus Name. Amen!

Chapter 17

God Calls Us Out

God calls us out. He called Abraham out of his country, from all he knew and said, "Go to a land I will show you." God called the Israelites out of Egypt. He walked with them in the desert until such a time as they were ready to accomplish the plans He had for them to conquer the Promised Land.

It seems when God calls us out, He doesn't always make the path perfectly clear. In fact, in the case of the Israelites, it seems the path became very circuitous because of their lack of obedience. I wonder how many times I've walked a path that was much longer than God intended simply because of my tendency to do things my own way, in my own strength and in my own time. Or, how many times God has called me out to watch me freeze on the threshold, because "out" is a scary place, full of the unknown and shrouded in mists through which I cannot always see.

I need to remember that what is unknown to me is known to God. When He calls me out, it's always to lead me to a better place - a place of blessing. "God is gently calling you from the jaws of trouble to an open place of freedom where He has set your table full of the finest food." Job 36:16. When He calls me out, He goes with me, even in the desert place. He asks me to take the step, not to worry about the path or figure out the outcome of the journey. Even when I'm not obedient, He's still there waiting for me to walk in faith; waiting for me to grab on to all He has for me. I remind myself of a toddler learning to walk, lurching forward, sometimes away from the very hands that will hold me up if only I will let Him.

So, when He calls me out and into the unknown, what's my job? My job is to walk, to go and to realize when He calls me into the unknown, He goes with me and He provides. I don't have to figure it all out. Abraham knew when he was called out and up to the mountain to sacrifice Isaac; it was up to God to provide. I need to know that and live it too.

Lord, help me to walk boldly into the unknown with You. Let me listen to Your call and be ready to get up and move via the leading of Your Holy Spirit. My earnest prayer is that if Your presence does not go with me; do not lead me up from here. But help me to also realize I may not know what every step of the way is going to look or feel like, but You do and that's enough for me. Let me be faithful to put one foot in front of the other. Help me to keep my eyes on You. I love you, Lord. Amen.

Chapter 18
Love the Unlovable

It's hard sometimes to love the unlovable; especially those who take advantage of you, use you for their own means and then dust their hands off as if to say, "Well, that's done." Jesus tells us in Luke 6:28,"Bless them that curse you, pray for them that despitefully use you." (American Standard Version) Early in my walk with Christ, I thought that sounded a little crazy. I wasn't sure it was something I would be able to do. But, the more I listen to the Lord and wrap my puny mind around the fact that His ways are not our ways, I learn everything He says is for my benefit and is intended to bring me into the abundant life He has for me.

So, I've been used, and made a fool of, or so it would seem. But, when I choose to pray for the person who used me, doesn't God actually fulfill another of His promises to me? "And we know that God causes all things to work together for good to those who love God, to those who are called according to His purpose." Romans 8:28 (New American Standard) First, God is using this situation for the good because it's an opportunity for me to react as a reflection of my Lord. Secondly, it's an opportunity for me to step into the realm of the spirit and intercede on behalf of the person who despitefully used me. It's my privilege to pray for this person to come to a saving knowledge of Jesus Christ. My prayer is that this will happen for him in a radical way. Leaving no doubt as to the power of God as He moves in this person's life. I'm asking for the miraculous to occur time and again and for the Holy Spirit to institute a heavenly campaign designed to turn this person to Christ in whatever way my Heavenly Father sees fit. (Visiting angels come to mind:) Thirdly, I have the opportunity to step out of the way and let the Lord fight my battles. In Exodus 14:14, Moses told Israel, "The Lord will fight for you; you need only to be still." Not easy in my humanity, trust me. But, I believe there's more blessing to be had by doing what I can do and then leaving the rest in God's more-than-capable hands. If Christ was able to pray for those who nailed him to the cross, surely I can pray for this person.

It's amazing how peaceful I feel. Of course, there was the initial shock and anger that someone would use people in this way, but I feel more sorrow for the person than anger actually, because what's at stake in this physical world is nothing to what's at stake for eternity. It saddens me because this person is busy scratching feverishly for a treasure that is going to fade away with no knowledge of Jesus Christ. My friend, if you ever read this, I pray you will come to know Jesus Christ as your Lord and Savior so you will learn the riches of this world are nothing compared to the surpassing greatness of knowing Jesus Christ as Lord.

Let's pray: Father, I thank you for the life lessons you allow us to walk through. They're not always easy. In fact, sometimes, they're costly and painful, especially when people despitefully use us. Yet, Lord, when You were used, You prayed and forgave. Help us to do the same. We want to be a reflection of You here on Earth. In Jesus Name. Amen.

Chapter 19

Is God Big Enough?

One evening while I was praying and worshipping I felt the Lord nudge me.

"Am I not the God of the Universe?"

"Yes, Lord, You are."

"Then why don't you trust me to do the things I say I will do? Did I not tell you, 'Greater things than these shall you do'? And am I not capable of doing them? Do you think you need to protect Me? That if you step out in faith and things don't happen the way you think they should somehow My reputation is damaged?" (It felt like He was chuckling as I "heard" this.)

"What I want is for my people to walk in faith and obedience. I want **you** to walk in faith and obedience. I will do the things I've said I would do. Miracles will follow those who are advancing the Kingdom of God, as proof that I am the God of the Universe. (Again, a chuckle.) Don't worry about Me. I can take care of Myself. What I need from you is to walk radically, saturated in the truth of my Word, ready to proclaim the Kingdom at any moment."

As I sat and processed, it seemed there was a little voice inside of me screaming, "You don't want to be too extreme! You can't rock the boat too much! People, even people in the church, will think you're weird and off-base and too 'out there'! "

Guess what? I think all of God's people who have done anything for the Kingdom have been extreme. Radically committed to the truth of the Word and willing to walk out the reality of the spiritual in the realm of the physical.

So, yes, Lord! Yes, I'm willing to walk radically and quit protecting You and Your reputation. I know You can take care of Yourself. (Obviously.) Let me see with Your eyes the divine appointments You have for me. Let me not only see them, but act in obedience and carry out Your Word, ready to show that the spiritual is more real than "reality." I love you, Lord!

Chapter 20

Out of the Blue

Have you ever felt God calling you to something, but you just didn't really feel qualified? In fact, you felt completely inadequate and totally unable to do whatever it was He was calling you to? (Think about Moses and the burning bush.) Well, I recently faced (and am facing) a situation like that in my own life.

I've been feeling that the Lord is calling me into a worship ministry. Not only singing backup vocals, but beginning to lead and *gulp* to learn to play a couple of instruments. You see, I'll sing all day long. I feel comfortable there. But to play an instrument is way outside my comfort zone.

So, I argued with God for about nine months. I can completely relate to Moses when he said, "Please, Lord, now send the message by whomever you will." Exodus 4:13. Meaning, send it by anyone but me. Still, the nudging persisted and I finally took the time to sit down and have a conversation with the Lord about it. The conversation went something like this:

"Lord, I'm feeling like you want me to learn to play guitar. And, well, You know I love to sing in worship. I'm just not really a musician. You know? I think You may have gotten the wrong person for this. I'll sing all day long, but the whole instrument thing is out of my league. We've got some really talented musicians on our worship team. I don't think we really need any more. So if this is really You talking to me, You're going to have to show me something 'out of the blue.'"

To make a long story short, two days later, a gentleman walked up to me at church carrying a guitar case and said, "God told me to give this to you."

Puzzled, I opened the case. Inside was a sky/turquoise blue guitar the likes of which I have never seen. (Nor am probably likely to see again!) It's almost neon in its "blueness." (In case you missed it, you need to remember I had prayed He would show me "something out of the blue.") Not only did He show me "something out of the blue," but He provided one of the instruments I had been feeling led to learn. I had to laugh, because I knew exactly what the Lord was saying. "Let Me worry about the outcome. You just be obedient and do what I'm telling you to do." Point, God.

As I laughed, I did have one more question for Him, "Really? You couldn't have gone with a navy blue, or something a little more subtle?" I could almost hear Him chuckle.

Now, when I'm out speaking and playing that guitar (in all my novice ability) I never fail to get comments about the guitar's color. As a result, I've had the opportunity to share God's sense of humor, and the work of His hand in my life, as I tell the story of how the guitar came to be with me. Each time I tell the story, it reminds me to be faithful to the path He has called me to walk.

Will I ever be a great and accomplished musician? I don't know. Somehow, I don't think that's really the crux of the matter. What matters is I am walking in obedience, doing what I can to be faithful to the gifts He has given me. The rest is up to Him.

Let's pray: Lord, I thank You for allowing us to have open conversations with You. I thank You for answered prayer and for being a very real part of our everyday lives. I ask You would help me to walk in obedience to You each and every day. I want to be faithful to walk the path You have called me to walk. I love you, Lord!

Chapter 21

It Won't Always Make Sense

Have you ever wondered what Noah was thinking when the Lord asked him to build the ark? And how about Abraham when the Lord told him to leave his country and relatives and go to a land the Lord would show him? I also think about Joshua commanding the Israelites to march around Jericho - not fight, but march and eventually shout. In all these situations, I can't help but think these guys probably had the same reaction we would have today. "But, Lord, that doesn't make sense!" Remember, they were flesh and blood just like you and me. The same doubts, the same fears, and the same humanity were just as much a part of their lives as they are yours and mine.

The Lord has been pressing some things on my heart lately that, to me, just don't make sense. Yet, He is saying, "Do this." I know I'm to step out into certain areas in which I love, but in which I don't always feel the most competent. So, in my mind, I wrestle with what I perceive to be the senselessness of it. I wonder if Joshua felt the same?

Still, I've come to the conclusion as long as it's not contradicting anything I know to be true about God and Scripture, why do I feel the need to "make sense of it?" Could it be I'm just to obey; to be like Nike and "Just do it?" Isn't that what Noah, Abraham, and Joshua did? They just did it and left the results up to God. I need to do that too. Even if it doesn't make sense to me, I know God knows the plans He has for me. And He knows the plans He has for you. It doesn't have to make sense to us. It only needs to make sense to Him. He sees our lives from a completely different perspective than we do. He knows how to work all things for our good.

So what is it that doesn't make sense that God is asking you to do? Are you going to do it? Take a step. Walk around the city and watch the walls fall down.

Let's pray: Lord, help me to walk in obedience. Help me to understand that things don't always need to make sense to me. You are God. You are in control. It's my job to walk humbly with You. Let me step out into the things You have for me, whether they make sense or not. In Jesus Name. Amen

Chapter 22

What's in Your Hand II

I wonder how many of us are "stuck" in a place God never intended us to be stuck, because we keep saying things like: "I'll be able to do more for God when....my kids are grown, my bills are paid and I have more money, I don't have to work this job, I have all the supplies that I need, or when I'm proficient in.....etc. etc."

God never asks us for what we don't have. He asks us to give Him what we do have (right now) and let Him make it enough. He asked Moses, "What is that in your hand?" to which Moses replied, "A staff." (Exodus 4:2.) He told the disciples, "You feed them." (Referring to the 5000 people who had gathered to hear Jesus teach.) And they said to Him, "We have only 5 loaves and 2 fish." And He said, "Bring them to me." (Mt. 14:17-18) Miraculously, the 5000 people were fed with what the disciples had available. In another instance, He told Peter to, "Cast the net on the right-hand side of the boat and you will find a catch." This, after Peter had been fishing all night without catching anything, but when he did as the Lord commanded, his nets were filled to the breaking point. (John 21:6)

I find it amazing and humbling that all God asks is for us to trust Him. He doesn't say, go get the job to get the money that will feed the 5000. He says, "Are you willing to give me what you have and allow Me to make it more than enough?"

So, what do you have? Time, talent, money, a house, a car, a gift of hospitality, the ability to write, draw, cook, fix cars, etc. Give Him what you do have. Because all He asks us for are the things we have in our hand, right now. When we trust Him with those things, He will always make them more than enough to accomplish whatever it is that He has called you to accomplish. Take the time to make a list of what you have that you feel God may ask you to use. Are you willing to allow Him to use it? Don't stay stuck. Give God what you have in your hand and allow Him to make it enough!

Lord, help us to trust you. Unstick us from our future focus and help us to understand Your desire to use what we have in our hand right now for Your Glory. Open our eyes and our hearts to everything You have for us, Lord. Let us serve You with all our heart, mind, soul and strength. In Jesus Name.

Chapter 23

Sustainer of My Soul

Behold, the Lord is my helper; the Lord is the sustainer of my soul." (Ps. 54:4 NASB)

I love this verse. I've been rolling it around in my mind and the utter vastness of it astonishes me. The Hebrew for Helper here (Azar) meant first to surround. But also to protect, aid, help, succor, support, give material or nonmaterial encouragement. And even to run to the aid of. The Lord is my helper. Wow. How can I even begin to describe how insignificant my problems are when I bask in this verse?

What do I ever have to be concerned about? The Lord is the sustainer of my soul.

The definition of sustain from dictionary.com means:

1. *to support, hold, or bear up from below; bear the weight of, as a structure.*

2. *to bear (a burden, charge, etc.).*

3. to undergo, experience, or suffer (injury, loss, etc.); endure without giving way or yielding.

4. to keep (a person, the mind, the spirits, etc.) from giving way, as under trial or affliction.

5. to keep up or keep going, as an action or process: to sustain a conversation.

6. to supply with food, drink, and other necessities of life.

7. to provide for (an institution or the like) by furnishing means or funds.

8. to support (a cause or the like) by aid or approval.

9. to uphold as valid, just, or correct, as a claim or the person making it: The judge sustained the lawyer's objection.

10. to confirm or corroborate, as a statement: Further investigation sustained my suspicions.

Mull over each piece of this definition as it applies to God being the Sustainer in your life. The ramifications are astounding!

God is the one who bears me up, who provides for me, who supports me, who keeps me going through the ups and downs of life. Yes, but I sense it's so much more. He is the very fabric of my being something so integral to my existence that without Him there is no life, no purpose, and no meaning.

Let's Pray: The Sustainer of my Soul, forgive me for being so easily distracted by the "problems" I encounter. Help me to trust fully in You. You are my helper. You are my Sustainer. With You to run to my aid, whom shall I fear?

Chapter 24
Looking Ahead

Have you ever had a time in your life when you began thinking about your past? More specifically, when you began to think about the mistakes, the failures, the could-have's and should- have's in your life? And have you ever noticed how it's so easy to jump from one failure to another to another until pretty soon you're miserable and feel like you've got nothing to offer?

I know I've experienced those moments. It's so easy to beat ourselves over the head with our mistakes. Yet, I notice God never does that to us. As a matter of fact, what I see in Scripture is a desire to continually point us to our future, not to our past; to restore us and do a new thing in our hearts and lives. If that's God's heart, restoration and redemption, who am I to dredge up my past? If I have been given the mind of Christ, then shouldn't I be thinking of myself as God thinks of me? (I Cor 2:16) "For who has known the mind of the Lord, that he will instruct Him? But we have the mind of Christ." (NASB)

Don't get me wrong, I'm not saying we don't have to work through past pain. We have to address issues of the past in order to step into the new life God has for us. If we don't address those issues, they'll simply fester and grow and manifest themselves in all manner of unhealthy (and ungodly) behavior. I'm talking about those issues we have dealt with but that we (or the Enemy) continue to dredge up and beat ourselves over the head with in unguarded moments. I don't think God minds failure as much as we do. I think He knows in our weakness, He is made strong. He is able to show His redeeming power in our lives through our mistakes and our failures.

So, what does God think of me? He sees me as I will be in Christ, conformed to the image of His Son. Any life circumstance, good or bad, He'll use to accomplish His purpose in my life if I'll let Him. God only ever uses my past to bring me into the fullness of my future. He always says, "I have so much more for you. I'm here calling you. I desire relationship with you. My heart's cry is redemption and restoration for all men." Scripture shouts this from its pages. God speaks it to our hearts. The question is, are we listening? More importantly, are we hearing what He has to say?

Let's pray: Lord, help us to deal with our past hurts so we can move from our pain into the fullness of Your redeeming love for us. Help us to accept the mind of Christ in us so we can begin to see all You have for us. We desire Your truth and Your presence in our lives each and every day. We love you, Lord. In Jesus Name.

Chapter 25

When Abraham and Sarah Laughed

In reading the story of God's promise of a child to Abraham and Sarah the other day, I had a light shone in a new way upon the tale. In Genesis chapter 17, the Lord is reiterating His promise to Abraham regarding he and Sarah having a son, the son God promised would be their child, not one through a surrogate servant. Genesis 17:17 says, "Then Abraham fell on his face and laughed and said in his heart, Shall a child be born to a man who is a hundred years old? And shall Sarah, who is ninety years old, bear a son?" (AMP) What struck me was Abraham laughed. I've always remembered Sarah laughed when she heard the news, (Gen 18:12 "Therefore Sarah laughed to herself saying...") and she was "busted" by God who asked why she laughed and if there was anything too hard or too wonderful for the Lord. But I never noticed Abraham laughed first!

Then, I believe the Holy Spirit turned a spotlight on Gen 17:19 for me, because I'm not always the brightest bulb in the box. God is continuing his conversation with Abraham, the verse reads, "But God said, Sarah your wife shall bear you a son indeed, and you shall call his name Isaac (Laughter); and I will establish my covenant or solemn pledge with him for an everlasting posterity after him." (AMP) So here's my light bulb moment. I think God chose Isaac's name (Laughter) to be a continual reminder to both Abraham and Sarah of their initial response to God's seemingly impossible promise they would have a son. They both laughed. (You know, chuckled a little in the "oh-wouldn't-that-be-nice-but-it's-not-likely-to-happen" kind of way.) And God probably smiled while thinking, "Yes, the son I give you will bring you joy and cause you to laugh, but I'm going to name him now, before that joy, in honor of your reaction to my promise. Then, every time you speak his name, not only will joy flood your heart because you have a son, but you will be reminded of when you chuckled at My promise and yet the promise was fulfilled."

It made me think, what promise of God might I be chuckling at today? Maybe I received the promise years ago, but I have yet to receive its embodiment. Am I remembering there is nothing too hard for the Lord, or have I resigned myself to thinking "it would be nice...but.....?" I know I have at least one physical reminder the Lord has given me regarding His promises and His call on my life. (See 'Out of the Blue' Chapter 20.) How about you? What impossible promise are you chuckling over? The Father understands. In fact, He might be doing a little chuckling Himself as He works His perfect plan in our lives.

Let's pray: Lord, help us to remember there is nothing too difficult for You. Renew our hope and revive our spirits. You always fulfill Your promises, even when we laugh because we just can't see how it could ever be done. Turn our laughter of disbelief into guffaws of joy as we see Your plan worked in our lives. We love you, Lord.

Chapter 26

Are You So Very Different?

A few months ago, while reading about Israel's deliverance from Egypt and their subsequent wanderings in the wilderness, I couldn't help but feel a little smug, and dare I say, self-righteous. As I was reading about God's powerful deliverance of His chosen nation, the miracles, the provision in the wilderness, the water, the manna, and all of His marvelous works on behalf of His people, I couldn't help but look down my nose a bit at how Israel came to the point of complaining and grumbling time after time on their journey. I was astonished quite frankly. I mean, after the Lord brings you out of captivity where you were making bricks and were in utter slavery, how can you have the gall to say, "We remember the fish we ate freely in Egypt and without cost, the cucumbers, melons, leeks, onions and garlic. But now our soul (our strength) is dried up, there is nothing at all (in the way of food) but this manna." Numbers 11:5-6 (AMP)

After reading this, I thought to myself, "Seriously! These people have got to be some of the most pig-headed and ungrateful people ever! Come on! Look at everything God has done on their behalf and yet they have the audacity to whine like little babies." To which God responded in my heart, "Are you so very different?" Ouch! But honestly, am I so very different?

I've experienced the hand of God in my life. Maybe not as dramatically as the parting of the Red Sea, but He has worked on my behalf. Right after those times, I'm on my knees promising to love and serve Him with all my heart, just like the Israelites. Then, as I journey on and things get tough, or they don't turn out the way I thought they should, or there's an unexpected turn of events, or someone messes things up or...you name it, I do complain. "Why me?" "How come this?" "Are You going to provide for me?" "This is really hard." "Oh, if only I could go back." etc. Whine. Whine. Whine. Sound familiar?

We're all on a journey with God. He works in miraculous ways in our lives, if we let Him. The trick is to remember the miracles after we've trekked a few miles, months or years away from them. It's not the miracles themselves that are important. It's the God of those miracles who should command our attention. He is in control of every situation and circumstance. The only thing to be gained by looking back is an understanding of how far God has brought us and how faithful and marvelous He's been on the journey.

So, since I'm not really any different from the Israelites, I think I'll just go put my self-righteous nose back in place and remember what the Lord has done.

Let's Pray: Lord, forgive me when I whine. When I forget the things You've done and how far we have come. Help me to keep my eyes on You. I want to move when You move and stay when You stay. I love You, Lord. Amen.

Chapter 27
Love Says No

I had an interesting conversation the other day regarding tolerance. The person I was talking to supports the alternative lifestyles and demanded I should too. When I said that I don't operate in that belief systsem, she said somewhat sarcastically, "I thought you Christians were supposed to love everybody." To which I replied, "I guess that depends on your definition of love. If by love you mean I have to agree with you and never say no because that's not what you want to hear, then you'll probably think I don't love you. But let me ask you this, do you always agree with everyone you love? If not, does that mean you don't love them?"

How ironic to be accused of being unloving by someone who was clearly "not feelin' the love" for me.

This is what I know about love. Love speaks the truth in bold humility. Yes, I realize I just wrote the words bold and humility in the same phrase. You see, true love doesn't say you're right just because you want to hear you're right, but neither does it condemn. That's what I mean by bold humility. Look at Jesus' example in Scripture. In John 4 he speaks to a Samaritan woman at the well. During the course of the conversation He speaks the truth to her. Look at verses 17-19, "The woman answered and said, 'I have no husband.' Jesus said to her, 'You correctly said, 'I have no husband'; for you have had five husbands, and the one whom you now have is not your husband; this you have said truly." The woman said to Him, 'Sir, I perceive that you are a prophet.'" The conversation then goes on to Jesus eventually revealing Himself as the Messiah. I believe when Jesus spoke the truth, He spoke it in love, possibly with a tinge of sadness in His voice at her state of affairs.

Look at another scenario in John 8 with the woman caught in adultery. An angry mob drags her into the temple and places her in the middle of the court stating she should be stoned according to the Law. Jesus' answer in verse 7 should give us cause for reflection. "He who is without sin among you, let him be the first to throw a stone at her." After everyone leaves, Jesus has a conversation with the woman in verses 10-11. "Straightening up, Jesus said to her, 'Woman, where are they? Did no one condemn you?' She said, 'No one, Lord.' And Jesus said, 'I do not condemn you either. Go. From now on sin no more.'" I believe this passage holds the key to having bold humility. You see, when we keep in mind we are all sinners saved by grace, we'll be less likely to throw the first stone. Does that prevent us from speaking the truth? No. The truth was she was caught in adultery, in sin. But mercy caused Jesus to pause, love caused Him to speak truth and grace caused Him to forgive. Shouldn't we do the same?

I know I'm gonna lose some of you right here. That's ok. I still love you. And you can feel free to pray for me. I think one of the battles we're facing as believers' addressing "alternative lifestyles" is we're afraid to be labeled. We're afraid to be called unloving, bigots, narrow-minded, right-wing fundamentalists, intolerant, or whatever else we might be called, for fear it will ruin our witness. Really? My question is, "Why the fear?" People can call me what they want, that doesn't make it true. (The religious leaders of Jesus time accused him of being in cahoots with the Devil!) We all, as believers, need to genuinely ask and be receptive to hearing and speaking the Truth in love.

I like to think about love like this. I, as a parent, love my children. Because I love my children, there are some things I won't let them do because the outcome would be harmful to them. For instance, you are not allowed to play in the street because you might get run over. You cannot eat the whole bag of candy, because you will get a stomach ache if you do. When I say no to my children I'm saying no because I love them. I want to protect them. But, my saying no isn't always popular with my kids. In fact, there are times when they protest vehemently. Yet, I don't waiver in my love for them. It's precisely because I love them I'm willing to draw the line and stand my ground. Our Heavenly Father is like this with us. There are some outcomes from which He would like to protect us. So, He says no. It isn't always well received, but there can be no doubt about His love for us. I John 4:10 -11 says this, "In this is love, not that we loved God, but that He loved us and sent His Son to be the propitiation for our sins. Beloved, if God so loved us, we also ought to love one another." (NASB)

True love is willing to take the heat. So, yes, my friend, I do love you. Just not in the way you expected.

Let's Pray: Lord, help us to love as You love – not condemning, not condoning, but speaking the truth, saying no when appropriate and standing firm even when it's not easy. We love because You first loved us. Let us bring the fullness of Your love to those around us, to those who may have never experienced a love like You have for us. We love You, Lord. Amen.

Chapter 28

Blessed to Be a Blessing

When I think about the many blessings my Heavenly Father has bestowed on me and my family, I often stop in thankful adoration. There is nothing I've done to deserve what He has given me. I can only hope and pray that I'm the best steward of this life and the things He has given me I can be. You see, I know when God blesses me, He intends it to be used to become a blessing to others. Whatever I have is not mine, it belongs to my Lord and Savior, Jesus, to be used for the furtherance of His kingdom here on Earth. Sometimes I forget that and I become like a little child who wants to hold tightly to the "thing" I have in my hands at the moment. "Mine!" I want to scream, when the Lord asks me to give something away, be it money, material possessions or time. But, it's not mine. It's God's. I need to remind myself of that every time the 2 year old inside me decides she doesn't want to share.

Paul says in 2 Corinthians 9:6-9 "Now this I say, he who sows sparingly will also reap sparingly, and he who sows bountifully will also reap bountifully. Each one must do just as he has purposed in his heart, not grudgingly or under compulsion, for God loves a cheerful giver. And God is able to make all grace abound to you, *so that always having all sufficiency in everything, you may have an abundance for every good deed*; as it is written, 'He scattered abroad, he gave to the poor, his righteousness endures forever.'" (NASB, italics mine.) When I read these verses what pops out at me is the thought I am to sow bountifully, which means a LOT. I'm not supposed to be frugal when it comes to the things of the kingdom. When I sow bountifully God will make all grace abound to me so I will have sufficiency in everything and have an abundance for every good deed. Notice, I have an abundance for every good deed, an abundance that is to be shared. I translate that to mean I am blessed to be a blessing. When God blesses me, I am to turn around and bless others. It's the original pay it forward plan. Verses 10-12 go on to say, "Now He who supplies seed to the sower and bread for food will supply and multiply your seed for sowing and increase the harvest of your righteousness; you will be enriched in everything for all liberality, which through us is producing thanksgiving to God." Ultimately, God should receive the glory when we use the blessings He has given us as He intended.

God loves to bless His children, just like you love to bless your children. Actually, I think God loves to bless us even more. Sometimes I think He would love to bless us so lavishly we can't even begin to comprehend it. Deuteronomy 28 talks about how God longs to bless His people when they walk in obedience to Him. I'd like to share a lengthy passage here, because if you're like me, you don't always look up all of the Bible verses listed in devotionals. So here it is, Deut. 28:2-14 from the NIV version:

2. "All these blessings will come upon you and overtake you if you obey the Lord your God:

3. Blessed shall you be in the city, and blessed shall you be in the country.

4. Blessed shall be the offspring of your body and the produce of your ground and the offspring of your beasts, the increase of your herd and the young of your flock.

5. Blessed shall be your basket and your kneading bowl.

6. Blessed shall you be when you come in and blessed shall you be when you go out.

7. The Lord shall cause your enemies who rise up against you to be defeated before you; they will come out against you one way and will flee before you seven ways.

8. The Lord will command the blessing upon you in your barns and in all that you put your hand to, and He will bless you in the land which the Lord you God gives to you.

9. The Lord will establish you as a holy people to Himself, as He swore to you, if you keep the commandments of the Lord Your God and walk in His ways.

10. So all the peoples of the earth will see that you are called by the name of the Lord and they will be afraid of you.

> 11. The Lord will make you abound in prosperity, in the offspring of your body and in the offspring of your beast and in the produce of your ground, in the land which the Lord swore to our fathers to give you.
>
> 12. The Lord will open for you His good storehouse, the heavens, to give rain to your land in its season and to bless all the work of your hand; and you shall lend to many nations, but you shall not borrow.
>
> 13. The Lord will make you the head and not the tail, and you only will be above, and you will not be underneath, if you listen to the commandments to the Lord your God which I charge you today, to observe them carefully,
>
> 14 and do not turn aside from any of the words which I command you today, to the right or to the left, to go after other gods to serve them." (NIV)

Wow. I realize that's a lot to take in. I've been reading and re-reading this passage for several months now. Clearly, God wants to bless us. Not only materially, but in our families, in our vocations, in every way, shape and form imaginable. Why does He want to bless us? Look at verse 10, "So all the peoples of the earth will see that you are called by the name of the Lord and they will be afraid of you." We are blessed so we can point to God as our Source, our Provider, and our Sufficiency. We are blessed so those around us know we are God's people, and we share those blessings because when we do, it will bring thanksgiving to God from those who may not know Him. We are blessed to be a blessing!

Let's Pray: Lord, help me to keep in mind I am blessed to be a blessing. Forgive me when I act like a 2 year old and cling to "things" selfishly. I want to be a blessing to others. I want to sow abundantly. Show me where to sow and what to sow, whether it's time, talents or money. Teach me how to be a good steward of all You have given me: materially, spiritually, and relationally. I want to proclaim to the world around me I am blessed only because I am called by Your name. In Jesus Name. Amen.

Chapter 29
Faithful Provider

Ever been going along in life thinking, I'm finally getting somewhere, things are starting to settle down and sort themselves out, when smack! Something jumps up and whacks you upside the head? Yeah. Not fun. I had that happen to me a while back. I had set some new financial goals and just started rolling along thinking, okay, I've got this; it's going to work... then all of a sudden I got a big, unexpected bill in the mail. Smack down times two! It literally took the wind right out of my sails. Ever been in a situation like this?

What I found so humorous, in the dry ha-ha, sense of the word is I had been praying and reading about how God longs to bless His children. I had been talking to Him about stepping out in faith and trusting Him for His provision. And then the rubber met the road. So what did I do? I had a minor freak out of course! Then I came across a passage of Scripture in 2 Kings 19 in which King Hezekiah has received a letter from the King of Assyria basically telling him he was doomed. When Hezekiah received that letter he went straight to God. This is what verse 14 says, "Then Hezekiah took the letter from the hand of the messengers and read it, and he went up to the house of the Lord and spread it out before the Lord." Verse 15 starts out saying, "Hezekiah prayed before the Lord…" Of course, he prayed specifically about his situation. What grabbed my attention was how Hezekiah went straight to God. Can I be honest with you? I was more than a little frustrated with myself because I know I should go straight to God too. I just looked at the circumstances and "forgot" for a moment Who it is that I serve. Seriously! You would think I'd catch on one of these years! So, I took my unexpected bill and went to God with it. My prayer was something like this: "Lord, we've been talking a lot lately about how You provide for Your children. I know I am to seek Your kingdom first and all these things will be added unto me. I don't have the wherewithal to pay for this bill right now and I'm not sure exactly what to do, but I know You do. Help me to trust in You. In Jesus Name. Amen."

After I prayed, it felt like God said to me, "This didn't come as a surprise to Me."

To which I replied, "That's great, but it did come as a surprise to me and I'm not quite sure what to do with this right now." As I went on about my evening, I sent a text to a dear friend who is a prayer warrior. We pray for each other regularly and send various prayer requests back and forth. My text to her said something like this: "Got a big, unexpected bill….I know God will provide. Just not sure how. Asking for prayer. Thanks."

The first words of her text response back to me were: "Lord, this didn't come as a surprise to You." Okay, God, I'm listening. Then and there, I laid my letter in the temple and decided God had it under control, although I couldn't see how I would possibly be able to come up with the money.

Two days later I got a call from a company that needed immediate help on a project. As in, it's Friday night can you be on site to work an hour ago? (I work as an independent contractor.) The money I made on that project more than covered the cost of the bill. God is faithful. It's me who needs some work. The funny thing is, I've seen God provide time and time again. I know He provides. You'd think I'd be past the freak out stage by now. He provided for me in college. He's provided for my family on numerous occasions. And He continues His provision today. Why do I forget so easily?

Paul says in Philippians 4:19 "And my God shall supply all your needs according to the riches of His glory in Christ Jesus." (NASB) God is more than able to supply all my needs. If He's supplying them according to His riches in glory in Christ Jesus, what do I have to worry about?

Jesus said it this way in Matthew 6:31-33, "Do not worry then, saying, 'What will we eat?' or 'What will we drink?' or 'What will we wear for clothing?' For the Gentiles eagerly seek all these things; for your heavenly Father know that you need all these things. But seek first His kingdom and His righteousness and all these things will be added to you." (NASB) I wonder if God shakes His head sometimes when He watches me do my little freak out thing. I know I would if I were Him.

Let's Pray: Lord, You are my Faithful Provider. You always have been and always will be. I'm sorry for those times when I freak out, because when I do, I'm showing a lack of faith in You. You've never let me down and I know You never will. Thank You for Your patience as I struggle to lean without reserve on Your promises. You are my Sole Sufficiency. I love You, Lord. Thank You for Your abundant provision. In Jesus Name. Amen.

Chapter 30

Psalm 51 - Repentance

I love Psalm 51. It starts out by saying," For the choir director. A Psalm of David, when Nathan the prophet came to him, after he had gone in to Bathsheba." Scripture is raw with our humanity. It doesn't put a shiny spin on the actions of our Biblical heroes and heroines. It tells it like it is in all its' gory detail. The reason I love Psalm 51 so much is it gives me hope. It shows me that no matter how far I've fallen if I am willing to repent, to turn 180 degrees and walk in the opposite direction, God is willing to meet me there. How utterly humbling that thought is to me. How wonderfully amazing is the love God has for me.

I'd like to walk through some thoughts that spring out to me as I read this Psalm. Bear in mind, David was a real man, with thoughts, feelings and faults just like ours. He was called "a man after God's own heart," and that's one of the reasons I believe he was able to write this Psalm after his humanity got the best of him. I can see myself in David's writing, maybe that's why this Psalm resonates with me.

David starts out by asking God to be gracious to him according to the greatness of His compassion. David's heart is yearning for God to blot out his transgression. David wants nothing more than to be washed from his sin. You see, when we're walking in relationship with a Holy God, we become keenly aware of those things we do that displease Him aka our sin. David says in verse 3, "For I know my transgressions and my sin is ever before me." Man, can I relate. Have you ever had your sin run a replay loop in your mind? Over and over and over again your failure runs a repeat, like a scratch in a CD. Then David says, "Against You, You only have I sinned and done what is evil in Your sight, so that You are justified when You speak and blameless when You judge."

You see, David knew he had disappointed God. There's nothing more devastating than knowing you've let down someone you love. David's broken heart acknowledged he had disappointed God. I know there have been times in my own life when I've let God down, when I knew better, but went ahead and did my own thing regardless. Thank God for His mercy!

In verse 6 David says, "Behold, You desire truth in the innermost being, and in the hidden part You will make me know wisdom." I can only imagine David's downfall started with some mental gymnastics. The kind we use to justify behavior we know is not pleasing to God, but we want to do what we want to do, we go ahead and do it anyway. Here in this verse, David acknowledges that God desires truth in the innermost being, not mental gymnastics, not justification of our actions, just truth. And God promises He won't refuse truth and wisdom to anyone who asks. (James 1:5)

David also knew this about God. God is more than willing to forgive us when we fail. His desire is for us to walk in a relationship with Him. He wants to restore us. That's why David says in verses 10 - 12, "Create in me a clean heart, O God, and renew a steadfast spirit within me. Do not cast me away from Your presence and do not take Your Holy Spirit from me. Restore to me the joy of Your salvation and sustain me with a willing spirit."

Verse 13 is one of my favorites. It says, "Then I will teach transgressors Your ways, and sinners will be converted to You." Strange verse to have as a favorite, you say? Here's why. When we fail, if we repent, God allows us the opportunity to turn and grow and cause others to come to know Him through and in spite of our human failings. To me, that is amazing! God not only allows do-overs, He planned for them by promising to take our broken lives and make them new. To put the cherry on top, He uses our blunders as opportunities for us to be real with others about what God can do with a messed up life!

Finally, David says in verse 16-17, "For You do not delight in sacrifice, otherwise I would give it; You are not pleased with burnt offering. The sacrifices of God are a broken spirit; a broken and contrite heart, O God, You will not despise." I believe David would have given everything he had to take back what he had done. Sometimes we make mistakes that are beyond huge. But there was nothing David could do – the eggs were already scrambled and there was no unscrambling them. What God wants from us when we've blown it is this; a broken heart and a contrite spirit. Nothing more. When we acknowledge we've made a mess and there's no way we can clean it up, God begins to move in His restoration power. He makes all things new. Does that mean we won't suffer the consequences of our actions? No. David lost the son that was born to him and Bathsheba. But God used the union that stared out in deceit and murder to bring Solomon to the throne of Israel. God takes our messes and turns them into something we wouldn't have even imagined. As it says in Romans 8:28, "And we know that in all things God works for the good of those who love him, who have been called according to his purpose."(NIV)

So, why do I love this Psalm so much? First of all, it's real. It says we do fail as people, even people of God. Secondly, it tells me there is hope when I have failed. David models to me through his own brokenness that I, too, can be restored to a right relationship with God, no matter how big my failure might be. Finally, when I am restored, God will use my failings so I can teach others about Him.

Let's Pray: Lord, I never willingly want to blow it, but I do. Thank you for David's honesty in his writings. He laid his life in all its messiness before You, so we could learn to do the same. I ask for You to create in me a clean heart and renew a steadfast spirit in me every day. Let me walk in Your ways. When I do stumble and fall, let me come to You with a broken heart and a contrite spirit, not empty promises or a plan to work my way back into Your graces. I know You don't work like that. Let me live my life transparently, so others may come to know You in spite of my shortcomings. You are the God of restoration. Restore me, Lord. I love you. In Jesus Name. Amen.

Chapter 31

All Your Heart

In Mark 12: 29-30 it says, "Jesus answered, 'The foremost is, 'Hear, O Israel! The Lord our God is one Lord; and you shall love the Lord your God with all Your heart, and with all your soul, and with all your mind, and with all your strength.'" (NASB) I wonder what that verse should look like in my life? I say I love God, and I do, but am I really giving it my all? The definition of all is: "the whole amount, quantity or extent of." Another definition says that all is; "the whole of one's possessions, energy or interest." It can also mean being the utmost possible of. Hmmm. So, do I really love God with *the whole amount* of my heart, mind, soul and strength? Am I straining to know Him with the "*utmost possible of*" every part of my being? Sometimes I wonder. You see, I'd like to say, of course, I love God with all my heart, mind, soul and strength, but I often find myself distracted by so many things. There's a bill that needs to be paid, a family that needs to be raised, a friend who could use my help, a ministry I'd like to help; supper to be put on the table and the list goes on. If all means the *whole amount of*, then what part of my whole is God actually getting as I live from day to day?

Don't get me wrong. Raising our families, being responsible citizens, and working in ministry are all good things. I just want to make sure I'm doing them in the right order with the right focus in mind. You see if I'm loving God with all my heart, mind, soul, and strength, then my life with all its' "stuff" will fall into place. That's why Jesus said, "Seek ye first the kingdom of God and His righteousness; and all these things shall be added unto you." Matthew 6:33 (KJV.) I don't know about you, but sometimes I struggle to keep that perspective. Not only do I struggle to keep that perspective, but there are times when I know that I'm not even remotely close to giving God *the utmost possible of* my heart, mind, soul and strength. Thank God for His grace! What would my life, 100% consumed by God, look like? I would imagine it would look something like the life Jesus lived when he walked here on the Earth. Boy, I want to be like Jesus!

You see, Jesus anticipated divine appointments because he lived this verse in every fiber of his being. Since He lived loving God with all His heart, mind, soul and strength, He couldn't help but touch the world around Him as He was going about the business of life. He met a woman at a well. He touched lepers. He opened the eyes of blind beggars. He healed the servant of the Roman soldier. You know the stories as well as I. (And, if you don't, may I encourage you to read the Gospels? There are amazing life lessons in those books!) Day in and day out, the love Jesus had for His Father, His commitment of His heart, mind, soul and strength, oozed from His pores onto a world desperate for the scent of a living, loving God. I am to do the same.

Paul says, "But thanks be to God, who always leads us in triumph in Christ, and manifests through us the sweet aroma of the knowledge of Him in every place. For we are a fragrance of Christ to God among those who are being saved and among those who are perishing; to one the aroma from death to death, to the other an aroma from life to life. And who is adequate for these things?" II Corinthians 2:14-16 (NIV) Thanks be to God that He has made us adequate in Christ! It's my job to continue to love God, focusing and refocusing until I am 100% consumed and the utmost of me is saturated by Him. God understands my humanity in all its distractibility. He also knows my heart and my desire to love Him with all my heart, mind, soul and strength. As I continue to push toward that goal, He will make me the sweet aroma I need to be through Christ. He will orchestrate those divine appointments in the everydayness of my life. I need only to love Him and look for the opportunities.

Let's Pray: Lord, my heart's desire is to love you with ALL my heart, mind, soul and strength. I want to walk like Jesus walked during His time on Earth. That's a tall order, I know, but something I want to strive to do. Lord, orchestrate those divine appointments. Open my eyes to them. Allow me to be the aroma of Christ to those with whom I come into contact. I choose to seek You first, now and always. In Jesus Name. Amen.

Chapter 32

Created In His Image

I have a confession. I like reading books about quantum physics theory. They fascinate me. The mathematics of quantum physics is way over my head, but the theory is amazing. No, I'm not a brainiac. I'm just curious about God's creation. I like reading articles and books that make me think.

I was recently reading an explanation of holographic images in a book called "The Divine Matrix." While I don't agree with everything in the book, the chapter on holographs gave me some food for thought. Here is how the book describes a hologram. "If you were to ask scientists to explain a hologram, they would probably begin by describing it as a special kind of photograph where the image on the surface suddenly appears three-dimensional when it's exposed to direct light. The process that creates these images involves a way of using laser light so that the picture becomes distributed over the entire surface of the film. It's this property of 'distributedness' that makes the holographic film so unique.

In this way, every part of the surface contains the entire image just as it was originally seen, only on a smaller scale. In other words, each fragment is a hologram. *If the original picture were divided into any number of pieces, each one – no matter how small- would still show a full view of the entire original image."*

To summarize, the book says, "In a holographic 'something,' every piece of the something mirrors the whole something." It was interesting that I came across this information during a time when I had been wondering what it meant to be created in God's image. I have the nagging feeling that we, as believers, are missing a significant piece of the puzzle when it comes to being created in God's image. So I was asking myself, if I am created in God's image, what ramifications should that have in my life? Here is the verse I'm talking about, Genesis 1:27, "God created man in His own image, in the image of God He created him; male and female He created them." (NIV) I was having a very hard time wrapping my brain around the fact that we are created in God's image. Obviously, we don't have an "image" of God at which to look. He isn't a physical being we can see and touch. The Bible clearly says, in John 4:24, "God is spirit, and those who worship Him must worship in spirit and in truth." (NIV) So, what does that mean for me? How am I "like" God if I was created in His image?

Think back to the holographic image for a minute. The summary states, *"In a holographic 'something,' every piece of the something mirrors the whole something."* Basically, there is the image of whatever the holograph is stamped on all the pieces of the whole. Could that be what God has done with us as humans? Paul says, in Romans 2:14-15 "For when Gentiles, who do not have the law, do by nature things required by the law, they are a law for themselves, even though they do not have the law, since they show the requirements of the law written in their hearts…" (NASB) That means every individual has the image of God embedded in their being, whether they choose to acknowledge it or not. There is a compass which has been placed in us that has been damaged by sin. Because the compass is damaged, without Christ it will never send us in a true direction. But the compass is there just the same, a part of the holographic whole. Wrap your brain around that one. If I know everyone is created in God's image, how should that affect my treatment of my fellow man?

I understand most theologians agree the image of God refers to the immaterial part of man; meaning we are spiritual beings in a physical body. Therefore we're like God in certain ways, although we obviously cannot be who He is. Here are some God-like characteristics we humans were created to reflect: We were given freedom of choice, the ability to reason, and the ability to create. We have a capacity for relationship and a desire to fellowship with others. We also have the ability to make moral decisions. We were created in righteousness and were to be holy like God is holy, until sin. Through the work of Christ on the cross, we can regain our holiness and become transformed by putting on the new self we gain in Jesus. Ephesians 4:24, "and put on the new self, which in the likeness of God has been created in righteousness and holiness of the truth."(NIV) We have the capacity for dominion. We have been granted authority. We experience emotion. We have the ability to love and show compassion. We seek wisdom and knowledge and are able to use this to learn, grow and change the world around us. The list could go on, but I want to stop here. Suffice it to say; when we look at ourselves being created in God's image, it has astounding ramifications.

Being created in God's image should affect how I view myself and how I view others. It should impact the way I live my life! I think the holographic image example was dropped in my lap so I had a way to wrap my puny mind around the vastness of the statement; I am created in His image. Wow. I like how The Message puts it, "God created human beings; He created them Godlike. Reflecting God's nature. He created them male and female...." Gen. 1:27. Yeah, reflecting God's nature. That's you and that's me, a little piece of the vastness of God. I want to reflect Him to the best of my ability. How about you?

Let's Pray: Lord, You created me in Your image. Help me to live as the image You created. Let me see others as You see them – stamped indelibly with Your image, whether they realize it or not. I want to reflect Your nature and Your glory Lord, that's why I was created. Teach me the best way to reflect You in all I do. Let me grow in all ways to become more like You. In Jesus Name. Amen.

Chapter 33
Shifting Your Paradigm

Your paradigm is your view of how things work in the world. Basically, it's the way you believe things are. The question is, is your view of the way things are the way God views them? I know I might have just put skid marks on your brain. But, think about it. Much of the time we think to ourselves, well this is just the way things are, or this is the way I am, deal with it. My question is is your belief what God says about your situation or circumstance?

Take, for instance, your own view of yourself. Most of us are able to point out every fault and flaw instantaneously. That's your paradigm. This is the way I am. I've been this way for years, there's nothing I can do about it. Or my family has always been this way, that's why I'm this way. What happens when your paradigm smacks up against God's truth? Who are you going to choose to believe?

Let me give you an example. I know a woman who struggles with a very poor self image. There's no doubt in my mind she loves God and has accepted Christ as her Lord and Savior. In fact, she ministers to many around her. However, during one conversation it became very clear to me that her poor self image was holding her back from becoming all God wanted her to be. So I asked her if I could share a verse with her and have her think about what it might mean in her own life. She said yes. The verse I shared was this, Psalm 139:13-14 "For you created me in my inmost being; you knit me together in my mother's womb. I praise you because I am fearfully and wonderfully made; Your works are wonderful, I know that full well." (NIV)

My question to her was, "Do you believe God's Word is true?"

Of course," she responded.

"Do you believe, as this verse states, God created you inside and out? That you are fearfully and wonderfully made?"

"Sure," she said.

"Do you believe as it says in the verse, God's works are wonderful?"

"Absolutely!" She looked a little puzzled.

"Then doesn't it stand to reason if God created you and His works are wonderful, that *you* are wonderful as a part of His creation?"

Here is where the paradigm door slammed shut. "Well, I'm not wonderful, really. I have a lot of issues I'm trying to work through from my past and ...." She stammered a little here.

"Wait a minute. " I cut her off. "What I hear you saying is you agree the Word of God is true, except as it applies to you, right?"

She looked startled, "No! That's not what I'm saying at all."

"Really? Because you just said you're not wonderful at all, although Scripture clearly states you are as part of God's creation. God can't lie. So what paradigm are you living in, yours or God's? Would you give that some thought over the next few days?"

I know, there are probably more than a few of you who are reading this thinking, "Wow, Jean, how about a little compassion here?" Believe me, I was very compassionate. Precisely because I do love her, I want her to begin to base her beliefs on the truth, not on some faulty tape that's been running in her mind for years. At some point, we need to declare by what paradigm we're going to choose to live our lives. If we, as believers, are sharing the Word of God, pointing to it as being infallible, then aren't we hypocritical when we ask others to apply it as a solution for the problems in their lives, but fail to believe and apply it to our own lives?

We all live in a paradigm box, a belief system we accept as being the reality in our lives. The problem is, most of the time our box isn't based on truth, it's based on whatever input we've received from the relationships and circumstances in our lives. If the input wasn't grounded in Biblical principles, it's probably not true. Yet, we become so comfortable with our boxes, we're reluctant to trade them for something else. Imagine a two year old clinging to a filthy blanket. The blanket really needs to be replaced. It's tattered, torn, and who knows how many nasty germs are tucked away in its' fabric. You know it's time for the blanket to make its way to the trash can, never to return again. Ever try to coax a blanket like that out of a two-year-olds' hands so you can replace it with something fresh and new? Try it sometime, and watch the reaction. You see, I think that's what happens with us when our paradigm box bumps up against God's. We're so comfortable in our paradigms that when our Heavenly Father wants to make a change, we cling to our box like a toddler protecting a coveted blanket. So we scream, "This is how I *am…*" God says, "I make all things new." 2 Cor.5:17 (NIV)

"I've been told I'm______________all my life." God says, "You shall know the truth and the truth shall set you free." John 8:32 (KJV)

"I've lived with these thoughts or beliefs for years." God says, "Be transformed by the renewing of your mind…." Romans 12:2 (NIV)

"I'm not worthy of love, acceptance, etc., __________________ " (You fill in the blank.) God says, "Behold, what manner of love the Father hath bestowed upon us, that we should be called the sons of God…" I John 3:1 (KJV) and, "In this is love, not that we loved God, but that He loved us and sent His Son to be the propitiation for our sins." I John 4:10 (NIV)

You see, we have a choice. We can decide God's paradigm for our lives is true and is the one we want to live, or we can cling to our ratty old one. It's up to us. So many times, I see brothers and sisters, myself included saying, "Yep, God's Word is true. I believe it....except when it comes to me, you have to understand there's a lot I've been through. It's just not easy to get over this stuff you know." Now, I understand there can and should be a healing process. However, I often see believers not even willing to begin to speak the truth of God's promises in their own lives. Or if they do, they do it with the assumption it's going to be a long and painful process, something they'll wallow through slowly. That may be the case in some situations. I understand we're all a work in progress. But the fact of the matter is, it comes down to deciding whether our reality for our lives is ours or our reality for our lives is God's as outlined in His Word. Do we want to hang on to our blanket or are we willing to give it to God so He can give us something new? Sometimes it's tough to let go, but when we do, we'll begin living the life God promised.

Let's Pray: Lord, help us to shift our paradigm to the one You have for our lives. Let us believe and live in the truths of Your Word as applied to us, right here and now. You said You came that we might have life and have it abundantly. Let us accept and incorporate Your promise into our lives today. Your Word is Truth. You are the same yesterday, today and forever. Let us live in the truth you have for us. In Jesus Name. Amen.

Chapter 34
Witnessing

In Christian circles we often talk about witnessing. We should go out witnessing. We should be a good witness to those around us. We should give witness to the preacher who shouts, "Can I get a witness?!" Have you ever experienced a lump in your throat when you hear the word…like, uh-oh, here we go, I hope they don't call on me? I never know what to say. When it comes to witnessing and testifying in the Christian realm, I think we've made it a lot harder than it has to be. For some reason, we seem to think we need to become theologians if we are going to be effective as witnesses for Christ. Will you allow me to take some of the pressure off? God never asked you to become a theologian. He asked you to share what He's done in *your* life. That's all.

Think about it like this. Suppose you're out watering your grass on a sunny spring day. An elderly woman strolls by on the sidewalk pulling a little luggage cart full of groceries. As she approaches the intersection, her cart bumps into an uneven piece of sidewalk causing it to tip. One of the bags shifts and an onion plops out and rolls a couple of feet into the street. About the same time the onion is rolling into the street, you hear a skateboarder coming down the sidewalk of the cross street where the onion has made its' escape.

The elderly woman leaves her cart on the sidewalk and steps off the curb to retrieve the onion. You glance over just in time to see the skateboarder turn to wave to some friends, crash into the old woman's cart and go flying headlong into the street right in front of a vehicle! The vehicle screeches to a stop, but not before it swerves and takes out the mirror on your car. You pull out your cell phone and call 911, while running to see if everyone is alright.

Let me ask you a question, after the police arrive and assess the situation, what do they typically do? Begin taking statements, right? And the statements are the testimonies of the people who witnessed what happened. They saw or experienced the event. Since you were in your yard and saw what happened you're a witness. When the officers come to take your statement about what just happened are you going to get a big lump in your throat and a little panic knot in your stomach? Are you going to freak out and say, "You mean I have to WITNESS!? I have to give a TESTIMONY about what I saw?! I have to tell you what happened? I don't have anything prepared! I didn't study! I haven't written anything down!" Sounds a little silly, doesn't it? Most of us are simply going to answer the officer's questions. You give your version of what happened and move on. No big deal.

Why is it then, we start to stutter and stammer when we're given an opportunity to testify to the work of God in our lives?

Most of the time, we get stressed out because we're afraid we don't know enough Bible verses or theology or we'll be asked a question we don't know the answer to and we'll look ridiculous. Did you feel that way when you were giving your testimony about the onion incident? No. You were simply recounting the events as you experienced them. You see, your testimony is your eyewitness account of the things you've seen God do in your life and in the lives of others. It's not subjective or arguable. It's what you saw or experienced. Period. People may want to argue that they see things from a different vantage point, and that's fine. Their vantage point doesn't nullify what you've seen and experienced. Whew! Does that take a load off or what?

In Acts 1:8, Christ calls us to be His witnesses, "but you will receive power when the Holy Spirit has come upon you; and you shall be My witnesses both in Jerusalem, and in all Judea and Samaria, and even to the remotest part of the earth." (NIV) Notice Jesus didn't say, "You shall become my Bible verse quoters, or you shall have a 3-point mini sermon in your back pocket ready to deliver at any time." Nope. He said, "You shall be my witnesses." Easy.

The great thing about being a witness is you are simply recounting what you've seen or experienced. You saw something and now you are telling about it. That's all Jesus asks us to do. Tell others about what you've seen and experienced as it relates to His involvement in your life. Our testimony comes from our witnessing the intersection of the spiritual realm with the physical realm in our lives. It's what you see and experience (or witness) at this intersection that's your testimony. It's your story and yours alone to tell.

Revelation 12:11 says, "And they overcame him because of the blood of the Lamb and because of the word of their testimony, and they did not love their life even when faced with death." (NIV)

So the next time someone brings up witnessing or sharing a testimony, don't freak out. Just share your eyewitness account of what God is doing in your life. It's your story. No one can take it away from you.

Let's Pray: Lord, help us to be your witnesses to the ends of the earth. Give us the boldness to share our stories about the things we've seen you do in our lives and in the lives of those around us. You never asked us to become theologians or scholars. You never asked us to have all the answers. You just asked us to be a witness, to testify of Your work in our own lives. Thank you for opportunities to do that Lord. We'll leave the rest up to You. In Jesus Name. Amen

Chapter 35

The Truth Shall Set You Free

Ever heard the phrase, "Familiarity breeds contempt?" Sometimes I'm like that with Bible verses or Scriptural truths. "Yep," I yawn, "heard that one before. Thanks for sharing." Thank God for His infinite patience!

A while back, during some very trying times in my life, I was asking the Lord to speak to me through His Word. This verse seemed to leap off the page. "You shall know the truth and the truth shall set you free." John 8:32 (NIV) I thought to myself, I've read that a million times. So, I prayed, "What are the truths I need to know, Lord, in order to experience the freedom You're talking about?" That's when I remembered "I am the Way and the Truth and the Life. No one comes to the Father except through me." John 14:6. (NIV) If I'm seeking the truth, and the truth will set me free, it looks like I should ultimately finding my way to Jesus. I know, it sounds simple, doesn't it? The problem is I've been indoctrinated by the saying, "The truth hurts." Honestly, I cringe a little when I read "and you shall know the truth and the truth shall set you free" verse.

In my mind, if I'm going to experience the truth, it's probably going to hurt. And face it; I'm not big on pain. Then, I came across an anonymous quote that puts it perspective, "The truth doesn't hurt, unless it should." So, why do I think I need to hide?

According to Isaiah 61:1, Christ came to proclaim freedom to the captives. It says, "The Spirit of the Sovereign LORD is on me, because the LORD has anointed me to proclaim good news to the poor. He has sent me to bind up the brokenhearted, to proclaim freedom for the captives and release from darkness for the prisoners…"(NIV) Hang with me here. Jesus is Truth. (I am the Way, the Truth, and the Life.) Truth (Jesus) came to proclaim freedom. You shall know the Truth (Jesus) and Jesus (the Truth) shall set you free. I believe this freedom comes because once I am grounded in Truth (Christ); I have access to every spiritual blessing in the heavenly realms. Scripture says, " [3] Praise be to the God and Father of our Lord Jesus Christ, who has blessed us in the heavenly realms with every spiritual blessing in Christ." Ephesians 1:3. (NIV) Now, if I have access to every spiritual blessing in the heavenly realms then that means I have all I will ever need in any life circumstance! Therefore, I truly am free; free from worry, free from fear, free to know the truth, etc. Is your brain in a pretzel yet? I love it when God connects the dots for me!

So what were the truths I needed to know in order to experience God's freedom? Well, at that particular time in my life, one of the truths was God never promised the journey would be easy, He only promised He would be with us each and every step of the way. I needed to allow God to be God of my circumstance, trust that He would be with me each step of the way and walk in obedience to Him. When we begin to recognize the truth in our lives and circumstances, we really are set free to live as God intended us to live, in utter dependence on Him. And that's the truth!

Let's Pray: Lord, You promise we shall know the truth and the truth shall set us free. We want to know truth, Lord, because we want to know You. You are truth. Thank you for the freedom Your truth brings us. Help us to live in Your truth and freedom every day. We want to help others do the same. In Jesus Name. Amen.

Chapter 36
Citizens of Eternity

I voted today as a citizen of the United States of America. It's one of the privileges I have living in this country, to participate in the democratic process. Citizenship anywhere comes with both privileges and responsibilities. Today, when I exercised one of the duties and privileges I have as a U.S. citizen, it got me thinking about what Paul said in Philippians 3:20, "For our citizenship is in heaven, from which also we eagerly wait for a Savior, the Lord Jesus Christ…" (NIV)

Legaldictionary.com defines a citizen as: "a person who by place of birth, nationality or one or both parents or by going through the naturalization process has sworn loyalty to a nation." Freedictionary.com says: "a person owing loyalty to and entitled by birth or naturalization to the protection of a state or nation. A resident of a city or town, especially one entitled to vote and enjoy other privileges there. A native, inhabitant, or denizen of a particular place." As a citizen of any place be it a town, a region or a country, I have certain privileges and responsibilities.

So what does it mean to be a citizen of heaven? First of all, it means my citizenship is of the eternal kind, unlike my citizenship in the U.S. When I cease to exist in the physical, so will my U.S. citizenship. However, my heavenly citizenship spans the gap between my spiritual and physical existence and it will continue when I'm no longer present in this body. I'm a citizen of eternity. That is amazing! It also means I may not fit in with all the customs and philosophies of the place I'm currently living.

Ever had non-believing friends or relatives look at you like you had two heads? Imagine that. We citizens of eternity should be a living example of continuous culture shock, because there are bound to be misunderstandings when it comes to the standards of conduct by which we're choosing to live. Look at Galatians 5:19-24 "[19]The acts of the flesh are obvious: sexual immorality, impurity and debauchery; [20]idolatry and witchcraft; hatred, discord, jealousy, fits of rage, selfish ambition, dissensions, factions [21]and envy; drunkenness, orgies, and the like. I warn you, as I did before, that those who live like this will not inherit the kingdom of God.[22]But the fruit of the Spirit is love, joy, peace, forbearance, kindness, goodness, faithfulness, [23]gentleness and self-control. Against such things there is no law. [24]Those who belong to Christ Jesus have crucified the flesh with its passions and desires." (NIV) No wonder there are times when we feel like we just don't fit in. We don't! That's because those who belong to Christ are citizens of the kingdom of heaven, our lifestyle is (or should be) very different from those around us who have no allegiance to our "country."

Finally, as a citizen of eternity, I'm an ambassador for my homeland. I need to keep in mind, as I go about my business, the people with whom I come in contact may never meet another Eternal Citizen. I might be the only example they ever get to see. I know when I travel as an American, I want to leave the best impression possible. As a citizen of eternity, I want to do even more than that. I want to point the way to a homeland, that like my earthly country, opens its' arms to all.

You see, as a citizen of heaven, I'm really just visiting this place called earth. My loyalties lie in the heavenly realms. This world is not my home.

Norman Vincent Peale puts it like this, "Know that there is no death, that all life is indivisible, that the here and the hereafter are one, that time and eternity are inseparable, that this is one unobstructed universe. We are citizens of eternity."

Let's Pray: Thank you, Lord, for my citizenship in heaven. Let me be an ambassador who is able to bridge the cultural gap and introduce others to the splendor of Your glory. I want to live to glorify Your name. Help me to keep an eternal perspective. In Jesus Name. Amen

Chapter 37

Send Me One Of Your People, Lord.

A few years ago, I was in a very difficult time of my life. Awash in a sea of emotions, it felt like I was caught in the current and continually being slammed up against the rocks. It didn't seem I was ever going to get my footing.

One morning after a particularly ugly encounter with a person in my life, I struggled to pull myself together so I could go about my day. I was working as a marketing communications consultant and had a business meeting I needed to attend, but I couldn't seem to stem the flow of tears. I felt crushed in the core of my being. I got dressed, put on my make-up and headed out the door, all the while giving myself an internal pep talk, "You can do this. Pull it together. You need to be professional." I'm sure you get the picture. In spite of my best efforts, I did break down in tears a couple of times on the drive to my meeting. During my drive, a good friend called. She could tell it wasn't a good day by my shaky voice. I gave her a synopsis of the situation around the lump in my throat and asked her if she would remember me in her prayers. Before she hung up, she asked me what I was going to do, to which I responded, "I honestly don't know. I don't think I can hear very clearly from God right now. It would be great if God would just send me one of His people. Preferably in a long white robe with a white beard to give me a 'Thus saith the Lord.'" We chuckled a bit and she promised to keep the situation in her prayers. I breathed my own prayer, "Lord, send me one of Your people," and continued my drive to the meeting.

When I got to the meeting place, I quickly ran to the bathroom to redo my make-up because I knew I probably looked like I'd been in a fight. I was right. My eyes were swollen from crying, and my nose was red and runny. (You know how you look when you've been bawling your eyes out.) So I took a couple of deep breaths and did the best I could with my make-up. Squaring my shoulders, I marched from the bathroom to meet my professional colleagues, praying that I wouldn't break down in front of them. I'm sure I looked a sight, but no one made mention of it as we did the introductions and began to get acquainted. I had never met either of these two women in my life.

A few minutes into our conversation, one of the women looked at me and said, "Can I ask you a question?"

"Sure."

"This may seem a little strange, but do you believe God can speak to people through other people?"

I'm not sure if I looked shocked or not, but you could have knocked me off my chair with a feather. I swallowed, "Yes, I believe God can speak to people through other people."

She looked at me kindly, "I'd like to share something with you I believe God wants you to know if you're okay with that. Take it for what it's worth."

Now, keep in mind, I had never met either one of the ladies. The woman then proceeded to give me a synopsis of what had been happening in my life (which was spot on) and speak about an upcoming meeting I was going to be having. She also lined out what was going to happen in that meeting. When she was finished, she said, "I'll be praying for you." I thanked her and we went back to our business meeting. As we shook hands before we left, the woman who had shared with me said, "Will you let me know how things turn out?" I told her I would and took her card.

Shortly after I finished with my business meeting with the women, I had the meeting of which she had spoken. Everything happened exactly as she said it would, right down to the smallest detail. I felt like I was watching a re-run of a movie of my life, only I hadn't lived it yet. Talk about déjà vu! God worked miraculously in this situation and soon thereafter, I felt like I had finally gained some traction in my world.

A couple of days later I called the woman, whose name was Esther. I let her know what had happened and that she had been correct about what she had shared with me during our meeting. I said, "First of all, thank you for sharing. You were right on with everything you said. So, I assume you're a Christian?"

I could hear the smile in her voice as she said, "I'm so glad! God is good. And I'm a Messianic Jew, actually." We exchanged a few more pleasantries and hung up with each other.

Later that night it dawned on me God had answered my prayer – literally! Remember I asked God to send me one of His people? He did. He sent me a Messianic Jew! Literally, one of HIS people. All I could do was bow my head in gratefulness, thankful I serve a God who lives in the moment with me each and every day.

I saw Esther a couple more times, but we never did do business together. I know God set our paths to cross in a divine appointment that day. That's the kind of God I serve.

Let's Pray: Lord, thank you for caring about my life in every circumstance. I love the fact You are a daily life kind of God who answers prayer; even prayers tossed about in casual desperation. I ask that You would answer the prayers of my brothers and sisters today in amazing "this can only be God" ways. In Jesus Name. Amen.

Chapter 38

You've Got Talent

Have you ever looked at someone and thought to yourself, "Wow, is he (or she) talented!"? I know I have, especially when that person operates in a similar ministry to yours. In fact, there are times when I get downright intimidated by the talented people around me and I start thinking, "What am I doing here? These people are far more talented than I am. Maybe I should just go do something else." Have you ever felt that way?

One day, when I was feeling particularly inadequate, after listening to a vocal solo by a very talented sister in Christ, I said to the Lord with a tinge of envy in my heart, "You know, she has a really beautiful voice. I mean, it's amazing! My voice sounds nothing like hers."

To which the Lord replied, "I know, because you're not her. You have your gifts and she has hers. Your job is to use the gifts I've given you. If I wanted you to be her, I would have given you her gifts. But I made you to be you. Just like a snowflake, I made every person intricate and unique. So there's no need to compete. Just be the best YOU you can be and don't worry about anyone else." God doesn't beat around the bush when He talks to me.

You see, I think it's easy for us to get wrapped up in the comparison game. However, when we do, we lose focus of what's important in our service to the King. God never said," I want you to be like so and so over there." God uniquely gifted you and said, "Go do something with the talent I've given you." If I don't have to worry about being as good as, or as talented as, or sounding like someone else, it leaves me a lot of time to concentrate on what God has asked me to do with what He's given me. If you think about it, it takes a lot of the pressure off. And it allows me to freely celebrate the talent the Lord has given to others around me. Why? Because not only do I *not* have to be like them, I was created *not* to be like them! So, when I hear a beautiful voice, see a great painting, or listen to a wonderful musician I can enjoy the gift they are bringing because of their uniqueness without having to feel that if I don't bring the same thing, my gift has less value. I just think, "Ah, one of Your snowflakes, that's beautiful!"

In the parable of the talents (Matt. 25:14-30), the master gave different amounts of money to each of his servants. Some were given more than others. But I think it's important to note that each servant was given something. The master didn't come to the guy at the end of the line and say, "Sorry, there's nothing left for you." Sometimes, I hear people say, "I don't have any talent." Or "I've really got nothing to give." Can I tell you, that's not true? Every one of God's servants is given something. It might not be a talent as our society defines talent, but each one of us is given gifts and abilities to be used in the service of the King. Maybe you can't sing, but you bake a mean chocolate chip cookie. Or you've never drawn a picture in your life, but you are an awesome mechanic. I don't know what it is that God has entrusted to you to be used on His behalf. What I do know is it's our privilege to use it in the service of the King!

Not only does God give what I call "natural" gifts or the things we equate to talent. He also gives spiritual gifts to all of His children. Check out I Corinthians 12. Again, I don't need to worry about what gifts people around me may have. I just need to operate in the gifts He has given me to the best of my ability. When we all begin to do so, can you imagine the impact the Body of Christ will have on this world?

So, what gifts has He given you, both in the natural and spiritual departments? How can you begin to use them for His glory?

Let's Pray: Lord, thank You for the gifts You've given to each one of us. Show us how to use them to further Your kingdom. I love that I don't have to envy someone else's gift because you created me to be me. I ask for the "me" You created to bring glory to Your name in every way I possibly can. I love You, Lord. Amen.

Chapter 39

Spiritually Starved Children

How many times do you eat each day? Three? Four? Or more? For people in America, it tends to be on the "or more" side of things. Not only do we eat regular meals, but we also have a few snacks in between meals just to tide us over. When we look at ourselves in the mirror, most of us are at least a normal weight, if not a bit on the plump side. Rarely would we even consider skipping a meal. The minute we feel the slightest hunger pang, we say, "I'M STARVING!" and head for the refrigerator.

I recently saw a picture of a starving child and it made me wonder, "What would my spiritual body would look like if I could see it in a mirror?"

You see, I think we're great at listening to our physical bodies, because our physical bodies are very insistent, when they want something; like food, for instance. But how good are we at listening to and nurturing our spiritual bodies? My concern is, spiritually speaking, we're a Body of starving children; children of God attempting to do the work of God without the benefit of nutrition. When a body, or a Body, is starving, it cannot function as it was meant to function.

How do we become spiritually starved children? We merely neglect the disciplines we know are necessary to feed our spirits. Peter said, "Therefore, rid yourselves of all malice and all deceit, hypocrisy, envy, and slander of every kind. [2] *Like newborn babies, crave pure spiritual milk, so that by it you may grow up in your salvation,* [3] *now that you have tasted that the Lord is good."* I Peter 2:1-3. (NIV) We are to feed our spirits just like we feed our bodies, on a daily basis. What healthy baby do you know who'll go days on end without eating? The minute a baby feels hunger, it's going to let you know. Sometimes at the top of its lungs! I wonder how many cries of hunger may have been voiced in the nursery of the Spirit that we never tuned in to?

So, how do we feed our spirit? First, we fellowship with God. In John 4:34 it says, "My food," said Jesus, "is to do the will of Him who sent me and to finish His work." (NIV) In order for us to know His will and do His work, we need to immerse ourselves in His Word and prayer, not just on Sundays or when we've got a spare minute, but on a daily basis. It's important to our spiritual well-being! I'm not a proponent of formulas that require you to have devotions at a certain time or in a certain way. But, it's not a bad idea to develop a routine that works for you, because we are creatures of habit. Secondly, we need to engage in praise and worship. Psalm 22:3 says, "[3] But thou art holy, O thou that inhabitest the praises of Israel." (KJV) God inhabits the praises of His people. Being in the presence of God is vital to feeding our spirit. He is our source. Think of your praise and worship as you plugging in to the power source for your life. Without the source, the lights don't come on. Finally, it's important for us to be part of the Body of Christ. We need to be around other believers who can help us grow and mature. Hebrews 5:11-13 says this, "[11] We have much to say about this, but it is hard to make it clear to you because you no longer try to understand. [12] In fact, though by this time you ought to be teachers, you need someone to teach you the elementary truths of God's word all over again. You need milk, not solid food! [13] Anyone who lives on milk, being still an infant, is not acquainted with the teaching about righteousness." (NIV) Being connected to a body of believers will challenge us to move from milk to meat. But before we begin to try table food, we have to make sure we're not starving in the first place. I think if we were half as diligent about feeding our spiritual bodies as we are about feeding our physical bodies this world would be a radically different place! I'd like to see that happen!

Let's Pray: Jesus, You said You were the bread of life. Lord, help us to feast on the food You feasted on in the spirit, which was to do the will of Your Father, who is our Father too. Show us how to develop our spiritual health, so we can be effective in Your service. Forgive us if we've been guilty of starving our spirits. Let us feel hunger for the things You have for us, Lord. In Jesus Name. Amen.

Chapter 40

Fire Shut Up in My Bones

In Jeremiah 20:9, Jeremiah says, "But if I say, 'I will not mention His word or speak anymore **in** His name,' His word is **in my** heart like a **fire**, a **fire shut up in my bones**. I am weary of holding it **in**; **in**deed, I cannot." Sometimes I feel this way. Like God's Word is a fire shut up in my bones. What a great word picture Jeremiah uses to describe the urgency and the passion of needing and wanting to share God's truths so badly that it feels as though you might burst. Like there is a raging forest fire in your soul that cannot be stopped no matter how hard you try.

Right now, as I'm writing, my mind is flooded with all the thoughts I would like to share with you. Sometimes they come in such a deluge I can't keep up. There are different verses of Scripture that have come alive in my life. Things I've seen God do. Words I've heard Him speak. Sermons I've heard that have ministered to me. People who have shared their experiences with me and impacted my life. Yep. It's like a fire shut up in my bones and I can't wait to let it out! In fact, I'm compelled to do so.

The hard part is not everyone understands the fire inside. Given the human condition, most people look at you like you're a little crazy if you attempt to describe what you're feeling, even family and friends. I did try to explain my compunction to a friend of mine, but quite frankly I was at a loss for words. All I could come up with was, "Gaaaahh! I have to let it out! I have to write and sing and speak. I can't stop it any longer!" He smiled somewhat condescendingly and said, "Well then, you gotta do whatcha gotta do." NO! It's not just that, it's MORE! It's that I NEED people to GET IT when I share it. But, I can't convey the fire behind the feeling adequately enough. I wish I knew another language with a word or phrase to summarize what I'm feeling. Sometimes I think if I feel this way, what must God feel when He wants to communicate with us?

So, I'm letting the fire burn. I'm asking for the appropriate times and venues to share. I'm asking to continue to be filled with a fiery passion that will ignite a desire in those around me. I want the world to know My God is a Consuming Fire!

Let's Pray: Lord, You placed this fire in my bones, the fire of Your Word and Your Truth. Help me to share your fire with those around me. I want them to experience You as a consuming fire in their lives. Let them come to know You through the flame You fan in me. Consume me completely! In Jesus Name.

Chapter 41

If Your Presence Does Not Go With Us

There's a song I love that says, "In Your Presence, that's where I am strong, in Your Presence, O Lord my God. In Your Presence. That's where I belong, seeking Your face. Touching Your grace. In the cleft of the rock, in Your Presence O God." You see when we are in God's Presence everything else pales in comparison. When we are in God's presence, we can't help but be changed from the inside out. It's a marvelous work God does in us when we take the time to be in His presence. Moses knew this. He spent time in the presence of God. When he did, Scripture tells us his face shone. (Exodus 34:29) There was an outward expression of an inward transformation. It also says in Exodus 33:11, the Lord used to speak with Moses face to face. Man, I want that! I want that not only for myself, but for the Church today. We need it, especially in our day and age. We need people whose faces shine with the light of God's glory, but we won't shine unless we've lived in His presence.

I've spent quite a bit of time lately making this next verse my prayer. I know I'm getting ready to move into a new phase in my life. I feel it. Sometimes it's scary. But when I remember Moses' prayer and make it my own, I know I can move forward into whatever the Lord calls me to do. Here's the verse, Exodus 33:15, "Then he said to Him, "If **Your presence does not go** with us, do **not** lead us up from here. " That's my prayer too. "Lord, if Your presence doesn't go with me, I don't want to go. I don't want to stand for one second outside of the plan You have for me. I don't want to waste any more time. I want to move when You move, stay when You stay and fix my attention completely on You." Sometimes that's easier said than done. Yet, my heart's desire is to make spending time in His presence my top priority. When I do, God's promise to me is for everything else to fall in to place. "Seek ye first the kingdom of God and His righteousness, and all these things shall be added unto You." Matthew 6:33 (KJV.)

What more can I say? I just need to be with Him, basking in His presence, and absorbing all He has for me. What does He have for you? Get into His presence and find out!

Let's Pray: Lord, I love You. I want to be in Your presence. I want to speak with You face to face as Moses did. You know my heart. You know that if Your presence does not go with me, I don't want to move an inch. You promise You will pour Your Spirit upon Your people. Please do so, Lord. Let us carry Your presence with us everywhere we go, so we can impact the world around us. I want Your name to be glorified in all that I say and do. In Jesus Name.

Chapter 42 Royalty

One of my favorite movies is, "The Princess Diaries" with Anne Hathaway. It's a spin on the normal Cinderella story, with an ordinary, somewhat inept, teenage girl finding out she's royalty and having to deal with all that entails. It's a rags to riches story. Many women dream of something similar happening to them at some point in their lives. They envision Prince Charming sweeping them off their feet and taking them to his castle where they live happily ever after. It might even be better if they didn't know he was a prince in the first place.

Here's a thought for you. Did you realize when you were adopted into the Body of Christ, you became royalty? You actually have your own rags to riches story unfolding everyday of your life as a follower of Jesus Christ! Well, you might say, I don't feel very royal at all. As a matter of fact, I'm quite grungy at the moment, thank you. Guess what? Just because you don't feel royal doesn't mean you're not part of the royal family. Your Father is a King! That means you're going to need to learn to live by a new set of expectations. Think about the "Princess

Diaries," remember the "princess lessons?" Although, Mia was born royalty, she had to learn royal behavior once she learned the truth of her situation. It didn't all come to her naturally, it took practice. It might be the same with you. You might need to "take some lessons," by getting around other believers who've lived the royal life a while to find out what the expectations are now that you're a child of the King.

One of the expectations, Mia found daunting was how public her life became when others learned of her new status. The same may happen to you. When others find out you're a Christian, you can expect to be treated differently. Don't let it come as a shock to you. Now, your life is under public scrutiny, and actions and words you might not have given much thought to before, become fodder for the paparazzi. (You know, your non-believing friends and family, who love to watch how you behave and bring it to your attention when it doesn't meet their standards of how a believer behaves.) Jesus said, "You are the light of the world. A city that is set on a hill cannot be hid…." (Matthew 5:14) As royalty, you will find yourself in the spotlight more often than you might have anticipated.

Another lesson Mia learned was that royalty follows different rules and protocols from the people around them. Many times there's a lot to learn in this area. For Mia it was everything from how to sit properly to how to address a crowd. There were many times she felt overwhelmed with all the lessons she was required to learn. Sometimes our journey with Christ can feel that way too, especially when we're just starting out. During her learning process, Amelia made mistakes along the way. We all do. Don't let it deter you from becoming the royal representative you were meant to be.

Finally, Amelia learned, as royalty, her life was not her own. Suddenly, she had a responsibility live sacrificially in order to lead the people of her country. The same is true for us. As children of the King, we must learn our lives are not our own. They are to be given in service to our heavenly kingdom, our new country, if you will. Our new position requires us to put others before ourselves. Paul says it like this in Philippians 2:5-7, "Have this attitude in yourselves which was also in Christ Jesus, who, although He existed in the form of God, did not regard equality with God a thing to be grasped, but emptied Himself, taking the form of a bond-servant, and being made in the likeness of men." (NASB) If our Savior was willing to give up His rights and privileges as the Son of God and take on human form for the people of His kingdom, we should follow His example and take into account the needs of those around us as children of the King.

By now you might be thinking. This royalty stuff sounds like a lot of work. I thought I was going to sit in a castle surrounded by riches, having servants at my beck and call. To which I would like to respond, "With great privilege, comes great responsibility." You are now a Child of the King, your home is more lavish than you could imagine. Its' streets are paved with gold! You're on temporary assignment as an ambassador of Christ. It's up to you to show this world how the "other side" lives. Paul said, "Only conduct yourselves in a manner worthy of the gospel of Christ…." (Philippians 1:27.) Conduct yourselves as Children of the King. The rewards are worth it!

Let's Pray: Lord, we are Your children. As Your children we are privileged to be part of the royal family. We ask for Your help in training us to represent You well. Let us behave like royalty here on earth, so when we get to heaven we are ready to rule with You. Thank You, Lord. In Jesus name. Amen.

Chapter 43
Walking In Authority

Philippians Chapter 2:5-10 says, "Have this attitude in yourselves which was also in Christ Jesus, who although He existed in the form of God did not regard equality with God a thing to be grasped, but emptied Himself, taking the form of a bond-servant, and being made in the likeness of men. Being found in appearance as a man, He humbled Himself by becoming obedient to the point of death, even death on a cross. For this reason also, God highly exalted Him and bestowed on Him the name which is above every name, so that at the name of Jesus every knee will bow of those who are in heaven and on earth and under the earth and that every tongue will confess that Jesus Christ is Lord, to the glory of God the Father." (NASB) It's my heart's cry to have this same attitude in my life as Christ had in His. A total surrender and emptying of Himself to the plan God had for Him.

It struck me as I was reading verse 6, "who although He existed in the form of God did not regard equality with God a thing to be grasped," how completely Jesus walked in the authority God gave Him. Does that sound weird? In our humanity, we struggle and strive to make it to the top of the heap. Sometimes we're even willing to step on others to get to a position of authority in our workplaces, homes or lives. Notice how very different Jesus' approach was. He did not regard His equality with God (His authority) something to be grasped. He had the freedom of possessing power without attaching His worth to it. Basically, he was so confident in who He was and His place in the Kingdom He had nothing to prove.

I'm a black belt in karate. There have been times in my life when people have wanted to fight with me just to fight, because they heard I was into martial arts. As a black belt, I do whatever I can to just walk away. Why? Because I know what I'm capable of and I have no need to prove myself. Most black belts would do the same, because they know what they can do, but they would prefer not to because people end up getting hurt. That's walking in authority without exerting your power. Thinking about that made me realize how much authority Jesus walked in and how much power He chose not to exert when it came time to become a human. It's humbling to realize He chose not to exert His authority on my behalf. He chose *not* to prove something so I could have eternal life. What a sacrifice!

Jesus also walked in obedience, even when it meant death on the cross! I know I struggle in the area of obedience. I balk, dig my heels in, question and basically act like a spoiled child at times. Thank God for His mercy! Jesus walked in obedience precisely because He knew what it was to be completely surrendered to His Father's authority. When I begin to acknowledge the complete authority of God in my life, I'll have an easier time walking in obedience. Why? Because I'll know with God in control, I have nothing to fear. So, when He asks me to do something, I'll do it, just like Jesus did, without question and in complete surrender. Easier said than done, I know, but I'll keep working on it!

I think when we begin to walk like Jesus walked, in our authority as children of the Most High God; we'll see change in the world around us. We won't be rattled by those who want to pick fights, because we'll understand true authority empties itself for a greater cause. We'll be seeking first the Kingdom of God, instead of worrying about the temporary accolades this present world has to offer. We'll understand our job is to be obedient whatever the cost and we'll leave the rest up to God. If we were to have the same attitude Christ had, can you imagine the possibilities?

Let's Pray: Father, I want to surrender completely to Your authority in my life. To walk in it, to breathe it, to not have to prove anything to those around me because I'm confident in what I have and who I am in You. I know I need to walk in obedience, Lord. The complete obedience Jesus walked in with You. Help me to walk with You like Jesus did. I love You! Amen.

Chapter 44

Could Worship Be Messy?

I was reading in the Old Testament a while back, just skimming really, and it dawned on me while I was skimming along just how messy worship was. I mean, think about it, there were animals being brought into the temple. I live on a hobby farm. Farm animals tend to "do their thing" when they need to "do their thing." Then, there were the people, probably hot and dusty from traveling to get to the temple. Now, add in the actual act of sacrifice and you've got a lot of commotion and a pretty big mess! It made me wonder if our worship has left the realm of "real" (the dirt, the sweat, the blood, and the commotion) for the realm of "pretty" (stained glass windows, hushed tones, and darkened interiors.) Not that pretty is bad, but if we reduce worship to pretty does it work in our everyday lives?

You see, I think God is a God of the nitty gritty. And I have a funny feeling He wants our worship to be part of the nitty gritty in our lives. Not just the Sunday, all dressed up and singing pretty part of living, but the "I'm in the trenches doing what I've got to do" part too. I don't think we think of worship as being in the trenches with us. Yet, if you read through Psalms, that's exactly where David's worship was, in the trenches with him. He moaned, he complained, he was angry and he was *worshipping* in every situation in his life! If you want to see worship meet life, Psalms is the place to do it. I'm sure that's why I love reading them so much. They are the conversation of a real worshipper, living a real life, worshipping a real God. It doesn't get much more transparent.

That's what I mean about worship being messy. I think messy is okay with God. As a matter of fact, I think it's more than okay. I think it's where He wants us to be. He wants us to worship every moment of our lives, through the good times and the bad. God is a god of intimate relationship. He wants us to be real with what's going on and not make ourselves all pretty when it comes time to "worship." He already knows what we look like when we get up in the morning, so we don't have to worry about impressing Him. We need to be concerned with worshipping Him.

What exactly is worship? I looked at several online dictionaries, Merriam Webster seemed to capture the essence of them all saying, "an extravagant respect or admiration for or devotion to an object of esteem." I would venture to say that worship would also include the actions which are driven by the extravagant respect or admiration for the object of esteem. I believe worship is an intimacy with God that allows Him into the messes of our lives. It's a relationship that is undeterred when it finds itself up to its' elbows in the blood and guts of living because we know our God is the Lord of Every Circumstance; which means we can worship in every circumstance – the good, the bad, and the ugly. Our extravagant admiration can be expressed in many ways and in every circumstance. Just look at David's expression of worship in the Psalms. When he was angry, he worshipped. When he was afraid, he worshipped. When he was depressed, he worshipped. Worship should never be limited to the "feel good" moments of our lives. It's meant to be integrated into our daily DNA and poured over our ordinary existence.

Let's Pray: Lord, let us worship You in spirit and in truth. Help us to saturate every moment of every day with our worship of You. Regardless of our circumstances, help us to worship You. You alone are worthy. In Jesus Name.

Chapter 45

Doing the Best that I Can

I was driving along the other day and I ended up behind a car that was going much more slowly than the rest of the traffic. Much more slowly. Grrr! I was at the end of a long day and I have to admit my thoughts were less than charitable. "Come on! Get a move on it! If you can't drive it, park it!" I think you get the drift. When there was finally enough of an opening in the traffic, I squeezed into the next lane and prepared to buzz around the slow moving vehicle. As I passed the car, I got a glimpse of the driver. She was a little old Oriental woman no bigger than a 10-year-old, peering through the space between the steering wheel and the dash. She looked like she was scared to death. As I drove by I felt the Holy Spirit nudge me. "She's doing the best she can." I love how God uses daily life to teach me the lessons I need to learn.

The gentle nudge of the Spirit got me to thinking, "Isn't it funny when I'm doing something I'm not comfortable trying or when life throws me a curve ball how I want people to show me grace and mercy. Yet, when I encounter someone else, like the woman behind the wheel, I get impatient and wonder what the problem is? How very human of me."

You see, we all want grace and mercy extended to us in our time of need; those moments in our lives when we're doing the best we can with the hand we've been dealt. Maybe we've lost the person who used to drive us to our appointments, or we've hit a financial brick wall. Whatever situation we may be facing, our hope is to be met where we are by a huge helping of grace topped off with a generous dollop of mercy. I know that's how my Heavenly Father meets me in all of my life circumstances. He knows I'm doing the best I can, so He extends His unfathomable grace and mercy to me time and again. I need to do that for the people around me; like the little Oriental ladies who are driving terrified down the freeways of life.

So, as I was getting off at my exit, I asked the Lord for forgiveness. Forgiveness for my impatient attitude and my lack of grace and mercy. Jesus gave us The Golden Rule, "Do unto others as you would have them do unto you." I want grace and mercy extended to me; therefore I need to extend it to those around me. My little Oriental woman will never know how she reminded me to walk as Jesus walked. But I did pray for her as I drove to my destination. I prayed first and foremost that if she didn't know Jesus as her Lord and Savior, she would come to know Him. I also asked for grace and mercy to be extended to her from the other drivers. I prayed, too, for her to reach her destination safely. Who knows? Maybe someday someone will be praying these same things for me.

Let's Pray: Lord, forgive me for the times I'm impatient and not showing others the same grace and mercy You extend to me every day. Let me be an extension of Your love to the people around me. Help me to keep in mind they are doing the best they can. In Jesus Name. Amen

Chapter 46

God is God, No Matter What

Though the fig tree should not blossom and there be no fruit on the vines, though the yield of the olive tree should fail and the fields produce no food, though the flock should be cut off from the fold and there be no cattle in the stalls, yet I will exult in the Lord, I will rejoice in the God of my salvation. The Lord God is my strength, and He has made my feet like hinds' feet and makes me walk on my high places." Habakkuk 3:17-19 (NIV)

Habukkuk isn't a book I spend a lot of time reading, but this verse seemed to jump out to me today. It looks like the author was living in some desperate and scary times. Sound familiar? What struck me about the passage was while the author acknowledges times are tough, he follows up with a small but powerful word - yet. "*Yet,* I will exult in the Lord. I will rejoice in the God of my salvation." (Hab 3:18) I love that passage. It says no matter what, I will exult in the Lord. Regardless of my circumstances, God is still the God of my salvation. Things might look scary and the world may seem to be falling apart around me, yet if God is for me, who can be against me? What do I have to fear? What do I have to worry about? I think it's important to keep this in mind as we listen to the news and go about our daily business. God is God, no matter what.

You see, it's easy to get caught up in the mainstream feeling of despair. However, we as children of God, are not like those who have no hope. And we know God has not given us a spirit a fear. As a matter of fact, Habakkuk says, "The Lord is my strength, and He has made my feet like hinds feet, and makes me walk on my high places." Hab. 3:19. Wow. If God is my strength what more do I need? You see, I think God has more in mind for us than we have in mind for ourselves, especially during trying times. Have you ever watched a mountain goat climb a mountain? They go where it looks impossible to go. One wrong move and it's over. *Yet,* (there's that word again) God makes our feet like hinds' feet (like a mountain goat) able to traverse places others wouldn't dream of attempting. But with God all things are possible, even making it through times or circumstances that appear impossible to overcome. I wish I were better at keeping this in mind when life heads my way like a semi truck careening out of control.

I need to remember that no matter how bleak things seem, my God is still on the throne. He's in charge. He is worthy of my praise and my exultation, especially during the trying times. Think about Paul and Silas, beaten, thrown into a dark dungeon, and shackled to prevent escape. Acts 16:25 tells us, "But about midnight Paul and Silas were praying and singing hymns of praise to God, and the prisoners were listening to them…" Oh, how I wish that were always my first reaction to ugly life circumstances! They acted out in the flesh what they knew to be true in the spirit. God is worthy to be exulted in any and every circumstance.

Let's pray: Lord, I ask You to show me how to live out what I know to be true in my spirit. You are worthy of praise in every life circumstance, no matter how bleak. I thank You for equipping me to traverse the high places and to go where not many others have gone. Let me boldly face whatever life may bring my way, knowing that through it all, You will be exulted. In Jesus Name. Amen.

Chapter 47

By Their Fruits You Shall Know Them

Matthew 7:18-23 states, "A good tree cannot produce bad fruit, nor can a bad tree produce good fruit. Every tree that does not bear good fruit is cut down and thrown into the fire. So then, you will know them by their fruits. Not everyone who says to Me, 'Lord, Lord,' will enter the kingdom of heaven, but he who does the will of My Father who is in heaven will enter. Many will say to Me on that day, 'Lord, Lord, did we not prophesy in Your name, and in Your name cast out demons, and in Your name perform many miracles?' And then I will declare to them, 'I never knew you; depart from Me, you who practice lawlessness." (NASB)

As I was reading this passage today, I was struck by the seriousness of what is being said. To have Jesus say, "I never knew you, depart from Me…" is a sobering thought. Sometimes I think we take our walk with God a bit too blithely. It's amazing to me how the verse states these people will be prophesying, casting out demons and performing miracles. Yet, sadly, they have missed the mark.

I believe God is all about relationship; an intimate, turn-your-life-inside-out relationship that continually causes us to become more like Christ. The more like Christ we are, the more fruit we will bear. Galatians 5:22-23 gives us the list of the fruits our lives should be producing. "But the fruit of the Spirit is love, joy, peace, patience, kindness, goodness, faithfulness, gentleness, self control; against such things there is no law." (NASB) Then in Ephesians, Paul says, "for the fruit of the Light consists in all goodness and righteousness and truth…" Eph. 5:9. Fruit is the visible evidence of our connectedness to Christ. An apple tree doesn't grow oranges. If He is the Vine and we are the branches, then our lives ought to be a reflection of the Vine of which we are a part.

Sadly, I've encountered, "Christians," who have left in their wake a swath of destruction and death. I've even been accosted by a few of them who were out to "set me straight" in some area or another. They have determined, in religious pride, that the way they have decided to live is, "The Way," period. But is it? Don't get me wrong, I believe we need to speak the truth in love with one another, but there is a big difference between walking in the fruits of the Spirit and operating in our own agenda. There's a difference between the black and white legalism that brings death, and the love of Christ that produces restoration and life. Fruit can't be faked. We can fake works, preaching, music, prophesy, and even miracles, but fruit is the outcome of whatever we are sowing in our lives. God clearly tells us we will reap what we sow. (Gal. 6:7) Which makes me take a look at the fruit in my own life. What have I sown? Have

I sown life? Do I have healthy relationships? Are people sensing in me the fruits of the Spirit? Do I minister to others in humility cloaked with compassion? Do I show love, joy, peace, patience, etc. in my interactions? I hope so. I know I don't always hit the mark. But, I thank God for His grace and mercy when I don't! My heart's desire is to live a life full of the Fruits of the Spirit, because "by their fruits you shall know them." I want to be known as a child of the Most High God.

Let's pray: Lord, You told us by their fruits shall we know them. Help me, Lord, to manifest Your fruit in my life. Let me produce the fruit of the Spirit so those around me can taste and see that the Lord is good. Because, You are good. I ask also Father, for those who may be deceived regarding what it means to follow You, that You would remove the veil from their hearts. Bring them into a vibrant relationship with You, so they too will bear fruit worthy of the calling of Christ. In Jesus Name. Amen.

Chapter 48

God Is Love

I know many of you have heard the phrase, "God is Love." The other day I was trying to wrap my brain around that. I John 4:16 says, "We have come to know and have believed the love which God has for us. God is love, and the one who abides in love abides in God, and God abides in him."

The question I had to ask after reading this was, "What is love?" Paul gives us the answer in I Corinthians 13:4-8, "Love is patient, love is kind and is not jealous; love does not brag and is not arrogant, does not act unbecomingly; it does not seek its own, is not provoked, does not take into account a wrong suffered, does not rejoice in unrighteousness, but rejoices with the truth; bears all things, believes all things, endures all things. Love never fails: but if there are gifts of prophesy, they will be done away; if there are tongues, they will cease; if there is knowledge, it will be done away."

I know most of us have heard or read the I Corinthians 13 passage on numerous occasions. This time, however, I decided to substitute God for the word love in the passage, since John told us in his writing, God is love. This is what it read, "God is patient, God is kind and is not jealous; God does not brag and is not arrogant, He does not act unbecomingly; He does not seek His own, God is not provoked, He does not take into account a wrong suffered, He does not rejoice in unrighteousness, but rejoices with the truth; God bears all things, believes all things, endures all things. God never fails..."

As I read through the verse with my substitution I thought about how everything rang true. God is patient. He is not willing that any should perish. God is kind and is not jealous. Were it not for the kindness of God, He would not have sent His Son to die on the cross for us. God does not brag and is not arrogant. God asks us to come to Him of our own free will, something that continually boggles my mind. He does not act unbecomingly or seek His own. Whatever God does in our lives is always for our good. It is always done out of a pure love with no agenda. I have a hard time comprehending that kind of love. He is not provoked or easily angered. Look at how He endured with Israel in their wilderness journey. Though they failed Him time after time, He never failed them.

Truthfully, I'm glad I'm not God, because I'm not sure how many people would actually make it past an offense! Which brings us to,"He does not take into account a wrong suffered." Boy, do I need to do more of this. Forgiveness is key. We need to be imitators of God in this area. Willing to move on after we have suffered wrong, knowing if God is for us, who can be against us? Then it says, God does not rejoice in unrighteousness, but rejoices with the truth. We too, need to rejoice in the truth and be as saddened by the state of our unrighteous society as our Heavenly Father is. God bears all things, believes all things, endures all things. God never fails.

John also says in I John 4:7, "Beloved, let us love one another, for love is from God; and everyone who loves is born of God and knows God." (NASB) Which I take to mean we need to become God-like in our character and live the definition of love spelled out for us by Paul in Chapter 13 of I Corinthians. That's a tall order! Yet, if we keep in mind with God all things are possible, we can cling to the hope of becoming the children He wants us to be.

Let's pray: Lord, I know You are the embodiment of love. You showed us what true love is by loving us first, before we could even begin to wonder what love was. I want to live a life of love Lord. But, it's not always easy in a world filled with anger, hate and fear. I know perfect love casts out fear, that You cast out fear. Show me how to walk in love like Jesus did. I love You, Lord. Amen.

Chapter 49
As a Man Thinketh

I have a quote on one of my file cabinets that says, "If you realized how powerful your thoughts were, you would never think another negative thought in your life." (Peace Pilgrim) Sometimes I don't think we, in the Christian world, take the time to understand how powerful our thoughts really are. Many times we just "poo-poo" the conversation regarding the power of our minds as some New Age mumbo jumbo we're far too spiritually sophisticated to address. But the reality is, there is a nugget of truth in some of the New Age philosophies. Proverbs 23:7 says, "As a man thinketh in his heart, so is he…" While this passage in Proverbs is talking about a selfish man being generous out of less than pure motives, I wonder if we could also apply it to our own lives..What we think tends to come to pass in our lives. When we expect and look for the worst, the worst seems to happen. When we expect and look for the best, the best seems to happen too. Talk about self-fulfilling prophesy!

Paul states in Philippians 4:8, "Finally, brethren, whatever is true, whatever is honorable, whatever is right, whatever is pure, whatever is lovely, whatever is of good repute, if there is any excellence and if anything worthy of praise, dwell on these things." (NASB) Notice he says to dwell on the positive. Dwell means to live in a specified place. I take that to mean we should be focusing on whatever is true, honorable, right, pure, lovely, of good repute, of excellence and worthy of praise in the humble abode of our minds. What a drastic difference this would make in our lives if we chose to follow Paul's advice!

I know in my own life there are times when it's just easier to let negative thoughts roll around unchecked, probably because they're familiar. Sometimes those negative thoughts are from the past, sometimes they're from recent developments, but the fact remains, they're negative! I have the ability to choose what I want to mentally chew on at any given moment in the day. However, most of us have never developed the discipline to stop thinking negative thoughts. We believe they just are, so we let them continue to wear ruts in our minds. Brothers and Sisters, we're supposed to be transformed by the renewing of our minds! "And do not be conformed to this world, but be transformed by the renewing of your mind, so that you may prove what the will of God is, that which is good and acceptable and perfect." Romans 12:2 (NASB)

I like the quote from Santosh Kalwar, "We are addicted to our thoughts. We cannot change anything if we cannot change our thoughts." Since Paul tells us we are to be transformed by the renewing of our minds, it seems obvious we should be looking to change our thought patterns. The question then becomes, "How do we do that?" Again, Paul provided us with the answer in Philippians 4:8 about the types of thoughts on which we should be dwelling. Just where are we to find those types of thoughts? I believe there are many resources: Scripture, devotionals, positive entertainment, worship music, conversations and association with uplifting people, etc. If we want to see change in our lives, it's up to us to take control of our minds.

I've had a couple of conversations with some people who declared they weren't thinking negatively, they were just "realistic." Now, I'm not a proponent of a pie-in-the-sky mentality, but I'm also not willing to buy into an Eeyore outlook on life. I chose to believe and to think what Scripture asks me to think, regardless of whether or not it fits easily into my present circumstances. If God says He causes all things to work together for the good of those who love Him and are called according to His purpose (Romans 8:28), then, I chose to dwell on that thought rather than how difficult my life might be right now. Notice, I'm not denying the difficulty, but I'm choosing to dwell on what God has stated as truth. Mark Twain put it this way, "Drag your thoughts away from your troubles...by the ears, but the heels, or any other way you can manage it." I chose to manage it by tapping in to the mind of Christ that God has promised to His children.

Proverbs 4:23 says this, "Be careful what you think because your thoughts run your life." (NCV) It's important for us to develop an awareness of the dominant thoughts roaming around in our brains. Are they in line with the Word of God or have we let some other programming preempt what God has for us? When it comes to the whole realm of negative thoughts, I often apply the verse, "The thief comes only to steal, kill and destroy; I have come that they may have life, and have it to the full." John 10:10 (NIV) If that's the case, if my thoughts aren't bringing me life, then I have to believe they aren't based in what God has for me and I need to tear them out by the roots and start with fresh seed.

Let's pray: Lord, help me to wrap my mind around how powerful my thoughts are. I want to be transformed by the renewing of my mind. To think as You would have me to think about myself, others and the world around me. Teach me how to dwell on the true, the pure, the things that are excellent and of good repute. Make me mindful when I'm allowing unhealthy thoughts to run amok and help me to show them the way out. Let me think thoughts that run my life along the paths You have for me. In Jesus Name. Amen

Chapter 50

Be All That You Can Be

If you live in the United States you've probably heard the slogan for the US Army, "Be all that you can be, in the Army." I think they had it right. At least the "be all you can be" part. I believe God wants us to be all we can be. We just aren't so sure about ourselves. We're quick to point out how weak we are, or the times we've tried and failed, or how we've made a mess of things on more than one occasion. Welcome to being human. It's a fact. We're going to mess up and fail and be weak and stumble and… the list goes on. The great thing is we serve a God of restoration. It comes as no surprise to Him when we make a mess of things. He knew what would happen before we did. Kind of like a parent watching a child attempt to take his first step. Most of the time he wobbles and falls down, but a loving parent will pick him up and encourage him to try again, because we know that's how the child learns. God is the same way. He allows us to try and possibly fall down, because He knows we will learn from it. He's always there to pick us up and encourage us to try again.

Oswald Chambers says it well, "Are you sufficiently right with God to expect Him to manifest His wonderful life in you? 'Nay, but we will serve the Lord.' It is not an impulse, but a deliberate commitment. You say – But God can never have called me to this, I am too unworthy, it can't mean me. It does mean you and the weaker and feebler you are, the better. The one who has something to trust in is the last one to come anywhere near saying – 'I will serve the Lord.'"

"We say –'If I really could believe!' The point is – if I really will believe. No wonder Jesus Christ lays such emphasis on the sin of unbelief. 'And He did not many mighty works there because of their unbelief.' If we really believed that God meant what He said – what should we be like! Dare I really let God be to me all that He says He will be?" My Utmost For His Highest.

I think Mr. Chambers hits the nail on the head. We need to deliberately determine to be all God means for us to be. In order to do that, we have to believe what God says about us and about Himself. Sometimes that's easier said than done. The question is am I willing to lay aside my opinions and well-entrenched dogmas about who I am and who God is in order to let Him reveal to me what the truth of the matter actually is? Again, easier said than done. Yet, if I want to be all I can be, I must step with abandon into whatever God is asking me to do or be. How about you? What is God asking you to do that is going to help you to be all you can be in His kingdom?

You know, soldiers go through rigorous training in order to make them fit for service. They must obey orders without question and place an unwavering faith in their commanders. They develop discipline, confidence and loyalty. They understand the importance of team work and are prepared to move out on a moment's notice. Could God be using our life circumstances as our training ground? Are we willing to give our all when we are called upon in the service of the King?

Let's Pray: Lord, I know you want me to be the best I can be. I want that too. Show me what I need to do in order to accomplish that goal, Lord. Let me rely on You as my sole sufficiency. I don't want to step out in my own strength or veer off in my own direction. I want to concentrate on what it is You want me to do, when You want me to do it. My heart's desire is to be all I can be in You, Jesus. Amen!

Chapter 51

A God of Miracles

I serve a God of Miracles. Not just the ones you read about in the Bible, but real, in today's day and age miracles. I've experienced them in my own life and I know other people who have experienced them too. So when people say, "Miracles aren't for today." I have to smile.

What miracles, you ask? Where should I begin? How about as a young teenager, when the Lord healed my eyes and I no longer had to wear glasses? Or the financial provision He orchestrated all throughout my college years? Or the time I had cracked ribs and could barely breathe, let alone move, and while I was attending a service the speaker stopped in the middle of his sermon and said someone here needs something in their side healed, God is doing that right now. I immediately felt heat go through the entire side of my body and when we were asked to stand and sing, I actually stood and sang without pain! There are so many more miracles I could share from my own life, but there are other miracles I'm aware of in the lives those around me I would like to mention. For instance, the Lord provided $2000 overnight for my daughter who was in Australia for discipleship training. She was supposed to leave for her field work, but didn't have the money and God provided. A friend of mine desperately needed help in the form of bodies to get work done on her house. A recently single mom, she also needed some groceries for her family. God was faithful and moved on the hearts of the members of a small local church who came to her aid. I love it when God shows up in our daily lives and interrupts us with a miracle!

I've had people ask me why I think we don't see more miracles today. Honestly, I believe it's because we don't expect or ask for them. If we're sick, we can go to the doctor. If we need money, we look to family or friends or government aid. If we need food…well, you get the picture. It's so easy in our society these days to look everywhere but to God when we are in need. And face it, a lot of time, we aren't in need in our culture. We've got jobs, food, housing, etc. What in the world would we need God for? So, we hum blithely along, wrapped up in our lives. Deuteronomy 8:11 says it like this, "But that is the time to be careful! Beware that in your plenty you do not forget the Lord your God and disobey His commands, regulations, and decrees that I am giving you today."(NLT) Sadly, we tend to turn to God only in the most desperate circumstances. Wouldn't it be better for us to walk in the expectation of having God work on a daily basis in our lives? Can you imagine what that would be like?

Sometimes I think I miss out on the miracles God has for me simply because I don't ask. There are many times when I set out to "figure things out" for myself. I wonder if God watches me with a sigh and thinks to Himself, "It would be so much easier if she would just ask Me first." I'm getting better about that, but I'm still not there. Yet, if I'm going to take God at His word, I need to keep in mind the words Jesus spoke, "I tell you the truth, anyone who has faith in me will do what I have been doing. He will do even greater things than these, because I am going to the Father." John 4:12 (NIV) Ask yourself, "What did Jesus do?" Of course He taught, but He also performed miracles. And then He said, we would do what He had been doing and even greater things! Miracles were part of who Christ was as the Son of God. They should be part of who we are as the sons and daughters of God. We need to expect them as a part of our existence here on earth. A tall order, I know, but one bursting with potential if you think about it. So are you ready to begin to expect miracles in your life and in the lives of those around you? Imagine what a change that would be!

Let's pray: Lord, I know You desire us to experience Your hand moving in our lives. Forgive us for the times when we quickly run to our resources instead of looking to You. I ask for You to interrupt us with miracles and "God Moments" in our lives. Let us be willing to quickly point to You and give You the glory in those times. You are the God of Miracles and there is nothing too hard for You! In Jesus Name. Amen

Chapter 52

Jesus With Skin On

We live in a world full of pain and need. Just look around you. Think about the people you know or people you may have heard about who are struggling in some way or another. Life is full of darkness. That's where we come in. In this world fraught with trials, we have the opportunity to become Jesus "with skin on" to those around us. What does that look like? It looks like you!

James 2:15-17 says, "Suppose a brother or sister is without clothes and daily food. If one of you says to him, 'Go, I wish you well; keep warm and well fed,' but does nothing about his physical needs, what good is it? In the same way, faith by itself, if it is not accompanied by action is dead." (NIV) We are the hands and feet of Christ to the world around us. We are representing God here on earth. When the crowds were hungry, Jesus fed them. When they were sick, He healed them. When they were searching for the narrow way, He pointed the direction. You see, we need to do more than go to church. We need to be the church outside its' stained glass windows. And quite frankly, there are times when that's very inconvenient! If I'm going to be Jesus-with-Skin-On, it means I'm going to have to be willing to not only acknowledge the need around me, but I have to be willing to do something about it when I can. I have to put some skin in the game, so to speak. James says we need to put our money where our mouth is where our faith is concerned. "In the same way, faith by itself, if it is not accompanied by action is dead." James 2:17 (NIV)

I have a girlfriend who exemplifies putting her faith into action. She is constantly on the lookout for practical ways to meet people's needs. She doesn't have a lot of money herself, yet I've seen her give sacrificially to be sure others won't go completely without. She may make a meal. Or organize donations for a family. She has done simple things like drop off a bag of toiletries. It might not seem like a lot, but I know she's ministered to many just by being willing to recognize a need and do what she could to meet it. To me, she is being Jesus-with-Skin-On. She puts her faith into action by meeting practical needs. I wish more of us would take the time to do what she does. She inspires me!

Being God's hands and feet on Earth, isn't always convenient. In fact, sometimes it requires us to act totally contrary to our human nature. It requires us to be unselfish and be willing to sacrifice time, money, space, possessions and whatever else God may ask of us. Jesus said, "Where your treasure is, there your heart will be also." Luke 12:34 (NIV) If you want to know where someone's heart is, just ask them to give up something or to do something inconvenient and you'll know pretty quickly what's important to them. I know there are times in my own life when I've seen a need and turned a blind eye even though I could have done something. And to be honest, most of those times were when it wasn't "convenient" for me. I can only imagine how disappointed my Heavenly Father must be with my selfish attitude when I turn and walk away.

So am I saying I'm supposed to meet every need I'm aware of? That I should give up all my possessions, and live like a monk? No. What I'm saying is I need to be more aware of those situations in which God is asking me to be Jesus-With-Skin-On and then I need to do what I can to the best of my ability with a cheerful heart. "...God loves a cheerful giver." 2 Cor. 9:7 (NIV) Maybe God is asking me to open up my house for a Bible study. Maybe I'm supposed to bring a meal to a worn out mom. Perhaps, I'm supposed to take time out of my day and help someone get to an appointment. Or provide a room for someone who's down on their luck. I don't know what it is God is asking you to do. But there are a million ways to live out your faith. If you're fresh out of ideas, just ask God what He'd like you to do. He'll be sure to let you know.

Let's Pray: Lord, please show me how to be Your hands and feet in a world desperate for Your touch. Lay on our hearts what you would like us to do. Give us practical ways to minister to the people around us. If we're supposed to drop off a bag of groceries or help clean a house or change oil, show us those things we can do to make a difference. Help us to be "Jesus-with-Skin On" so the world will see You in us. In Jesus Name. Amen.

My Manifesto

I KNOW…

I know that I would rather die defending the ground where my Lord tells me to stand, than to abandon my post for something easier. I know I would rather run boldly into the dark along a path that I cannot see than stand immobile when my God tells me to go. I know I would rather live in a box, than have all the riches of the world if my Lord shows me there are people in boxes who need to know Him. I know I would rather be split in two on the altar of sacrifice than remain silent about His love ~ no matter how 'politically incorrect' I may be.

I will be called many things...extremist, bigot, intolerant, phobic, conservative, fundamentalist, crazy, freak, religious, dreamer, etc. Call me what you will. This world is not my home. My mission is to live in an intense spiritual reality; a spiritual reality few will understand and even fewer will embrace. The student is not greater than the Master.My Master gave everything. Can I do any less?

About The Author

Jean Peterson is a multi-passionate entrepreneur, motivational speaker and author with a thirst for the chaos os creation. She lives with her husband in their Tiny Home/RV traveling to the beat of a different drummer. A creative communicator, Jean seeks to present eternal truths in various mediums including speaking, writing, art, music and photography. Her passion is to give hope for joy, affluence, kindness and love with every encounter while encouraging others to LIVE the abundant lives they were meant to live.

Visiting with their adult children and grandchildren across the country is one of the greatest blessings of the gypsy life they're embraced for the foreseeable future.

Find her on Facebook at

https://www.facebook.com/jean.peterson.794

Or use her digital business card to get in touch:

jemopeterson.thebumpcard.me

www.ingramcontent.com/pod-product-compliance
Lightning Source LLC
LaVergne TN
LVHW010914110826
845149LV00013B/2355

* 9 7 8 0 9 8 9 6 1 1 7 2 5 *